Only Believe

By Paul F. Taylor

Just Six Days Publishing

Published in the USA by J6D Publications, PO Box 7, Toutle, WA 98649

shop@justsixdays.com

http://www.justsixdays.com

ISBN: 978-1523961085

Created with CreateSpace.com

Contents

Commendations for this Book

As a pastor of 26 years, I appreciate Paul Taylor's emphasis on not only the Bible's authority in all apologetics, but it's necessity as the starting point (presupposition) to all Christian ministry. This book reflects the heart of such an apologist. **David Martin, Pastor, Heritage Bible Church of Puget Island, WA**

Finally, a book written from a Spirit-filled perspective that profoundly centers our focus upon the truth of God's Word— not contingent upon facts and figures, but based upon the sheer majesty of who God is. With Only Believe, Paul Taylor offers an apologetic that does so much more than stimulate the mind regarding the existence of God. But it will build in you the faith necessary to possess the promises of scripture despite how you feel, what you think, or the obstacles in the way. **Kyle Winkler, founder and president of Kyle Winkler Ministries, and author of Silence Satan. (www.kylewinkler.org)**

"The Bible says so." Try giving that answer to a 21st century individual and get ready for them to be underwhelmed. Why? Because they have no idea the

enormity or power of that statement. We sing the song as kids, but somehow as adults we forget that the most authoratative and simple answer is, "The Bible tells me so." In his book Only Believe, Paul Taylor delivers the background to this profound answer. Read it for yourself and BELIEVE. **Eric Hovind, founder and president of** Creation Today.

It is my hope and prayer that you use the tools that God has given you with Paul's book. **Sÿe ten Bruggencate, Absolute Apologetics,** *presenter of the movie* How to Answer the Fool

Foreword

By Sÿe ten Bruggencate

Apologetics is easy, believe your Bible. That's the title of a talk I gave to a group of evangelists just prior to the atheistic "Reason Rally" in Washington D.C. in 2012. We are commanded to be able to give a reasoned defense of our faith, but all too often well-meaning Christians are duped into presenting a defense which is outside of, or even contrary to Scripture. Not so with Paul Taylor's book "Only Believe." One thing you will notice with this book is that it is packed with Scripture.

As Paul notes in his book, he and I come from different theological backgrounds. With how our differences are labelled it would appear that some of our theologies are worlds apart. An odd thing happens when we lay out the arguments for our respective positions though, we are far closer than the labels would indicate. Why is that? Because we both ground our positions in the Word of God. I recall with fondness one particular discussion where at first we thought our positions were entirely different only to discover that they were, as near as I can remember, identical.

As Christians, the Word of God is our ultimate authority and as the Apostle Paul writes to Timothy is "profitable for doctrine, for reproof, for correction, for instruction in righteousness."Why then do so many of us appeal to another authority to defend our ultimate authority? With "Only Believe" Paul not only lays out a Biblical defense for appealing to Scripture, but does so using some passages that I had not considered in the years I have taught the subject.

How refreshing it was to read Paul label as "irrelevant" an argument which opposed what God said in His Word.

In attempt at insult, a professed atheist chided me for never abandoning my Biblical presuppositions when presenting a defense of my faith. As you will read Paul was similarly chided by a far more famous professed atheist for the same thing. After reading "Only Believe" you will be equipped to be blessed with such an intended insult. It is my hope and prayer that you use the tools that God has given you with Paul's book.

Jesus Christ is King. He's my King, he's Paul's King, He's your King. We need works like this that teach us to recognize the kingship of Jesus Christ when we defend our faith in the hopes that the lost may come to know our King as their Savior.

Preface

Apologetics is wider than creationism, but creationism is most definitely a subset of apologetics. When I am defending the truth of Genesis, I am defending the foundational book of the Bible, so I am engaging in apologetics. In my opinion, creationism is a particularly relevant part of apologetics, because it is arguably the most frequent point of attack on the faith.

Over my many years in creation ministry, however, I began to notice that many of the most well-known apologists did not even take a creationist position. Not only that, but I began to be tired of my own argumentation that creationism should be given an equal platform with evolutionism in educational establishments. While there are those, who would view progress along that road as a good thing, I began to wonder why I was wanting the truth of God's word to be "elevated" to sit alongside a lie. As a consequence, I fell into arguments, where I would give my evidence for disbelieving evolution, to be countered by arguments for disbelieving Genesis. The frequent suggestion was that the creation / evolution debate was simply a debate between two beliefs. I might hold that my belief was true, but to what effort was I prepared to go to proclaim the truth of the Bible, and oppose other views as errors?

My association with *Answers in Genesis* began to change that mindset. I began to see that we needed to show Christians first that proclaiming the truth of Genesis was a necessary part of our faith. Through that ministry, I first picked up a copy of a book called "Always Ready", by the late Dr Greg Bahnsen, that showed that the secularized methodologies of Classical Apologists, who seemed to be the overwhelming majority, were not just ill-advised - they were actually unbiblical.

Consequently, my method of responding to the many phone call inquiries that I received when working at Answers in Genesis (UK) began to change. I no longer wanted to try to prove to these callers that the Bible was true, by using external evidences, as I had previously done. Instead, I took a firm line on the inerrancy of Scripture, and attempted to demonstrate that creationist arguments were a natural corollary of that position. As you, gentle reader, might have expected, my conversations began to have more authority, because this was no longer my authority, but the authority of God's Word.

When I came to the United States in 2011, and co-presented *The Creation Today Show* with Eric Hovind, I soon came across an apologist from a very different theological background to my own, called Sye ten Bruggencate. I think that we were both surprised that the other had so strongly adopted a Presuppositional approach to apologetics. Over the years, I have come to value Sye's firm approach to the subject, in which he suffers no fools gladly. I no of no other Presuppositional Apologist so strongly committed to the street presentation of the Gospel - so much so that he should really be described as an apologist-evangelist. And I have urged him many times to write a book, setting out his approach to the subject. God willing, one day soon he will do so. In the meantime, I am delighted an privileged that he has agreed to contribute the Foreword to my effort. What the reader would not realize is that Sye also became an unofficial editor, helpfully correcting my typos, grammar and spelling mistakes. Any remaining mistakes, however, whether linguistic or theological, are entirely my responsibility.

In compiling the material for this book, 13 chapters emerged, which form the complete argument and methodology of my approach to apologetics. The appendix, which is a written version of my talk about Richard Dawkins's book The God Delusion, is not really part of the substance of the book, but is included here, because I wanted it in print, and this seemed to be the most suitable book, in which to include it.

01 Introduction

Mark 5:35-36

While He was still speaking, some came from the ruler of the synagogue's house who said, "Your daughter is dead. Why trouble the Teacher any further?" As soon as Jesus heard the word that was spoken, He said to the ruler of the synagogue, "Do not be afraid; only believe."

Only Believe

There is a lot to say about believing in the fifth chapter of Mark's Gospel. From verse 21 onwards, we have two concurrent events. These events are often expounded separately, but I think we need to understand the impact that these events had on each other. The events are:

- Jairus requesting healing for his 12-year-old daughter
- The woman with an issue of blood being healed when she touched Jesus' cloak

During my prayer time a couple of weeks ago, it was as if God was telling me to concentrate on writing. This was not difficult for me to hear, because I like writing, and had a number of projects on the go. But it seemed to me that God was telling me to write a book called *Only Believe*. I knew that this phrase had to do with the healing of the little girl of the synagogue ruler, but I couldn't remember the reference or the context. So I started to read and study and pray and meditate.

This book is the result of those deliberations. I will expound all of Mark 5:21-43, but I am going to start with these simple two words from Jesus: "Only believe".

There is so much misunderstanding about belief, and the related concept, faith. It is a term both misunderstood and, for that matter, ridiculed. This ridicule comes not only from people of no faith, but also comes from those that, on the surface at least, appear to be of the Christian faith. For that reason, we ought to examine some of the phrases used by those who misunderstand what it means to believe.

Seeing is Believing

The old saying "seeing is believing" is well-known and equally well-quoted. When I say it is well-quoted, I really mean that it is frequently   quoted, not that it is quoted well! I have no doubt that many of you reading this book now will, like myself, have said this very thing – especially to our children, when they were fabricating stories.

That fount of all knowledge, Wikipedia, has a very brief, but apposite, definition of the phrase.

> **Seeing is believing** is an idiom first recorded in this form in 1639 that means "only physical or concrete evidence is convincing". It is the essence of St. Thomas's claim to Jesus Christ, to which the latter responded that there were those who had not seen but believed. It leads to a sophistry that

"seen evidence" can be easily and correctly interpreted, when in fact, interpretation may be difficult.[1]

As the Wikipedia editor has rightly commented, the saying owes much to the incident in John 20, when Jesus had appeared, after His resurrection, to the disciples, except that Thomas was not with them. On hearing the news, Thomas simply could not believe it. This incident is so important to our discussion in this book, that I will reserve space later to expound John 20 in detail. For now, it is sufficient to note that this attitude of Thomas did not turn out well for him, so we should assume that John 20 can actually be cited as a refutation of the phrase "Seeing is believing".

Wikipedia goes on to comment that the idea that seen evidence can be both easily and correctly interpreted is false. Indeed, their sister website, Wiktionary, gives a very useful quote on the subject, from a 19th Century work entitled "Guesses at Truth" by the brothers Julius Charles and Augustus William Hare.

Seeing is believing, says the proverb. Though, of all our senses, the eyes are the most easily deceived, we believe them in preference to any other evidence.[2]

Are the eyes "the most easily deceived"? I suspect this is probably the case, because sight is the sense upon which we rely the most. Yet the Bible frequently warns us that we should not trust this form of evidence.

We look not to the things that are seen but to the things that are unseen. For the things that are seen are transient, but the things that are unseen are eternal. (2 Corinthians 4:18 ESV)

An equally popular saying to the one in the heading is the rhetorical question "Do my eyes deceive me?" This is said when something unusual is seen. In such circumstances, where this exclamation might be used, the answer to the question would often be "yes, your eyes do deceive you". We are all used to the concept of optical illusions. The whole basis of these amusing puzzles is that our eyes can and do deceive us on numerous occasions. I remember driving to a well-known spot on the A719 highway close to Ayr in Scotland. There is a point on this road, where you can stop your car, facing uphill. You then release the brake, with the car in neutral, and it is able to start freewheeling uphill. What is the mysterious force that pulls your car uphill? The answer is gravity. You see, the uphill road is not really uphill at all. It is actually downhill, and a spirit level placed on the tarmac paving will prove the point. But the lie of the surrounding land causes an optical illusion, such that what is really downhill appears to be uphill. Your eyes are deceived.

What Is Your Evidence?

The request for evidence is a frequent request of the Christian, and especially the creationist. On one level the question sounds fair. After all, one of my frequent challenges to evolutionists is to produce evidence for their position - a request which I know will be impossible for them to fulfil. The reason why it will be impossible for the evolutionist to supply me with evidence is due to the nature of evidence and the nature of questions. The nature and use of evidence will require an entire chapter later in the book. For now, we simply need to observe that evidence requires a foundational worldview with which to interpret it. The saying goes that "evidence speaks for itself". It does not. Readers of detective fiction will know this only too well, how they can be misled by the inclusion of evidence early in a story, which leads them in one direction, only for a twist in the interpretation of that evidence finally to lead one to a different conclusion. What might be more pertinent for the moment is to look briefly at the nature of the question itself.

Most questions have a presupposition behind them, which colors the question, and restricts the possible answers that can be given, if the question is to be answered directly. Indeed, it is often possible for the presupposition behind the question actively to preclude a truthful response.

To illustrate this point, let us look at a very famous example.

Suppose George is asked "Have you stopped beating your wife yet?"

The form of the question suggests that the answer should either be "yes" or "no". But there is a presupposition behind the question. The presupposition is that, at some point in the past, George has beaten his wife. But, if George has never beaten his wife, and would never dream of doing so, then it is impossible to answer the question directly. Instead, George has to tackle the presupposition, otherwise the truth is obscured by it. Clearly, one way to do so might be for George to be indignant in his response, though his protestation that he has never beaten his wife might also be taken as a response to his own feelings of guilt. On the other hand, he might stop to offer evidence that he had never beaten his wife. Yet, this second method invites refutation of the evidence that he has offered, and counter evidence could be provided. Moreover, the offering of evidence by George that he has not beaten his wife concedes that there is a case to answer. Any evidence offered supposes a neutral platform on which to offer evidence, but the questioner does not ask the question from a neutral platform, but rather from a presupposition that wife beating has, at the very least, been a part of George's past. The most logical course of action is for George to highlight the presupposition, showing that the question is not neutral, deny the presupposition, and then demonstrate that the corollary of the presupposition is absurd.

Christians have spent a long time trying to provide answers for specific questions. Their reason for doing this is that they would suggest that 1 Peter 3:15 requires them to provide answers. But this is not strictly correct. This passage in 1 Peter 3 needs greater expansion later, but for the moment let us notice that some translations use the word answer and others the word defence. So the answer provided does not have to be a specific answer to a specific question. Rather, it is a defence of our position. Sometimes, the answer for the reason for the hope within us is not a direct answer to the question posed, but rather an answer to a more fundamental question underlying the question posed. One of the things we will be looking at in this book is the most biblical way to answer questions.

Why Do You Ask?

Adults who deal with children, such as parents and teachers, are very familiar with this question.

One teacher tells a tale like this.

Mary approaches the teacher, shyly.

"Sir?", she begins. "Would you punish a student for something she hasn't done?"

"Of course not!" is the reply.

"That's good!" exclaims Mary. "I haven't done my homework."

Parents soon learn that, when their children can talk, there may be reasons behind what they say.

One day, I was preparing food in the kitchen. My eldest daughter, Gemma, was 5 years old and my eldest son, Adam, was 2. Gemma came running into the kitchen.

"Daddy, Daddy, Daddy! Adam is standing on the coffee table!"

Now, the coffee table had a glass top, and we were definitely making sure that the children did not stand on it. So, I followed the little girl to the lounge, lifted my son off the coffee table, and told him off. Then I returned to the kitchen.

"Daddy, Daddy, Daddy! He's on the coffee table again."

I returned to the lounge, and this time Adam got a little smack. Yet, there was something odd about this scenario, so, I hid just round the kitchen door, where I could see the children. And, once she thought I was out of sight, that little monkey picked her toddler brother up and put him on the coffee table, and then ran to the kitchen shouting. "Daddy! He's on the coffee table again!" Indeed he was! But there was a very good reason why he was on the coffee table! His big sister had put him there.

"Da...ad!!? Have you got any of that stuff for filling in holes in the wall?" asked one of my children one day. What was the best reply? I could have answered "No", if I didn't have any. Actually, I did have some, so I could have answered "Yes". However, what I actually said was "Why do you ask?" You can probably guess the rest. Somehow, the child had got a screwdriver, and had wanted to see what happened if it was punched through the sheet rock. Now this is a book about faith and apologetics, not child-rearing, so I don't need to dwell on the outcome of that event. The point is that the correct reply was "Why do you ask?", because that question reveals the presupposition behind the original question. Another of the things we will be studying is how to find the presuppositions behind what is said.

---

[1] Wikipedia article, < http://en.wikipedia.org/wiki/Seeing_Is_Believing >, accessed 2014-11-01

[2] Hare, J.C. and A.W. (1848), *Guesses at Truth*, < https://archive.org/details/guessesattruthby00hareiala >

02 Only Believe

Jesus had three things, briefly, to say to Jairus.

1. Do not be afraid.

2. Only believe.

3. She will be made well.

Item 1 was negative. This is what Jairus was not to do. Item 3 was telling him what the outcome would be, that the prayer on behalf of his daughter would be answered. So item 2 was the only action that Jairus was required to undertake. Jesus told Jairus to believe. But that is not the whole of it. Jesus told Jairus to *only* believe. Nothing other than belief was required. Nothing other than belief was expected. Nothing other than belief was to be done.

We must educate ourselves constantly in biblical exposition to remember that our study requires context, context, context. So the phrase "Only believe" might well be a simple command. But we need to understand the context in which the command was given. In order to understand the context, we need to start further back. Our studies could begin almost anywhere. However, Mark and Luke agree that the sequence of events is as follows:

1. Jesus cast out the multiple demons from the Gadarene man.

2. Jairus came to Jesus, along with a multitude of others.

3. Jesus paused to heal the woman with the issue of blood.

4. Jesus continued to Jairus's house and healed his daughter.

The Healing of the Gadarene Man

The healing of the Gadarene man would require a lengthy exposition itself, in order fully to understand the event. And if we undertook such an exposition, then we would have to examine the previous passage, in order to obtain context. This chapter cannot become an entire commentary on the Gospels, so we have to start somewhere, and I am choosing to make just a couple of pertinent points about the healing of the Gadarene, which will become significant for the subsequent reports.

The story so far is that Jesus has met a demon-possessed man. He, or rather one of the demons, refers to himself as "Legion", because "we are many". Jesus casts out the demons, who go into a herd of pigs, which then rush into the lake and drown. Why were the people of that locality herding pigs?

Now there is an issue to do with why there were pigs, and this could easily become a bunny trail, so I need to address the issue to eliminate it. There are some who express concern over why Jewish people were keeping pigs. After all, pigs were considered unclean animals under Mosaic Law. Jewish people should certainly not be eating them, nor really touching them.

However, other people have discussed whereabouts this event took place, suggesting that these people were probably Gentiles. This does not eliminate the problem, though, because the land was clearly associated with Israel, so the prohibition on keeping pigs, whether by Jews, or by Gentile neighbors, would be the same. My reason for this short diversion is to underline the fact that there was a significant problem that the people of this region were keeping pigs, and this can be considered to be a spiritual problem, while, clearly, we live in a post-Acts 10 world, where keeping pigs is not an issue anymore.

The main point of the story, with which we should be concerning ourselves now, is the issue of Jesus' authority. The evil spirits who were tormenting this poor man had considerable power. We know this, because the locals had obviously tried to chain this man up, but the shackles were always pulled apart. Now it is easy to overlook matters here. Was this man highly muscular? Probably not. If he had been a first century Mr Universe, then the locals would probably not have tried to shackle him, nor would they ever have succeeded in getting the shackles on in the first place. So the man was probably no more than a normal man in appearance - apart from possibly not being clothed (Mark 5:15) - so that it was natural for the locals to make the attempt to shackle him. Again, the context suggests that they succeeded in shackling him, but that he subsequently pulled the chains apart.

This is somewhat similar to an Old Testament figure possessed, not by demons, but by the Holy Spirit - the man Samson. If you use Google images with the word Samson, you will get lots of Sunday School illustrations showing a huge muscular man. Yet the people in the book of Judges were constantly trying to find out where Samson's strength came from. When I was in High School, there was an older student, who we all referred to as Tug - I don't even remember his real name. Tug was big and thick set. Someone made the mistake of attacking him once, and he simply lifted his would be assailant off the ground, with just one hand. But we never asked him where his strength came from! We could see where his strength came from! It was in his huge muscles! Yet the people had no idea where Samson's strength came from. Therefore, I assume that Samson was probably quite a weedy-looking man. His strength came from the Holy Spirit.

In an analogous manner, the Gaderene man's strength was not his own - it was caused by the many demons who controlled him. These demons were very powerful. These demons also had knowledge. They were able to confess something that Jesus' disciples were mostly not quite ready to own themselves yet - that Jesus is the "Son of the Most high God." They also knew that their lot was to be tormented, but they were afraid of being tormented before the end of the world. For that reason they begged Jesus to let them possess the pigs.

This last request proves that the demons did not have the authority of Jesus. They could not voluntarily leave the man and possess the pigs. They had to ask permission from Jesus to do this. It is also clear, therefore, that Jesus could have refused them such permission. It was therefore the Son of God's Sovereign choice to allow the demons to leave the man and enter the pigs. I have no idea why Jesus allowed them to go into the pigs, and destroy them, rather than sending them straight to the pit of Hell. The reason why Jesus did this is not actually the point of this account. The point of the account is that Jesus had (and has) authority.

There are some people who seem to think that Jesus was a form of conjurer. One conjurer in Britain - a man called Derren Brown - has reproduced apparent miracles, in a television special called *Messiah*. This includes apparent "Christian" miracles.[1] Brown is a committed atheist, and used the show to try to provide evidence for his belief that there is no God. The inference made, though not given explicitly, is that Christians are gullible, and simply following evidence which is no evidence. Yet the Bible also gives examples of convincing false reproductions of genuine works of God. The similarity between the strength of the Gaderene demoniac and Samson would be one. The miracles produced by Pharaoh's magicians, in response to miracles performed through Moses, are another example.[2] I am making this point to show you that the miracles of Jesus were not there as a form of evidence for the existence of God. They are, instead, a demonstration, or outworking, of the divine authority of Jesus Christ, the Son of God. The miracles do not prove that Jesus is God. The demons did not need to see a miracle, in order to know that Jesus was God. It is the other way about. Because Jesus is God, it is to be expected that He will do miracles, because of His authority. I have labored this point, because I need to refer to it, as I move on with expounding this passage.

As I suggested earlier, there is a lot more that can be said about the account of Jesus driving the demons out of the Gaderene man. But it is not this section that I am concentrating on. I simply want to use the context, to help expound the account of the healing of Jairus's daughter. The context is that of the authority of Jesus, because Jesus is God.

Perhaps, in view of the previous paragraph, one final comment must be made about this account. I want to refer to the final conversation between Jesus and the healed, former demoniac.

And when He got into the boat, he who had been demon-possessed begged Him that he might be with Him. However, Jesus did not permit him, but said to him, "Go home to your friends, and tell them what great things the Lord has done for you, and how He has had compassion on you." And he

*departed and began to proclaim in Decapolis all that Jesus
had done for him; and all marveled.[3]*

Even in this section, I cannot expound everything. I simply
want to pick up on a fascinating connection. Jesus told the
man "Go and tell what great things the Lord has done for you."
Luke's Gospel has it that Jesus said "...what God has done for
you. As both Mark and Luke are reporting the same thing,
Mark is understanding the reference to "the Lord" to be a
reference to God. Yet this man goes away and "began to
proclaim... all that **Jesus** had done for him". (Emphasis added).
The account in both these Gospels joins the statements with
the word "and", not the word "but". The inference is clear.
The man was doing as he was told. Jesus told him to go and tell
what the Lord God had done for him, and the man is therefore
witnessing to the fact that Jesus is God.

The Woman with the Issue of Blood

I am going to skip over Jesus' initial contact with Jairus for
just a moment, to highlight the miracle that Jesus performed,
while on his way to Jairus's house. There was a woman, who
was seriously ill. In today's society, her illness of continual
menstrual or related bleeding, for 12 years, would be bad
enough. It would be an unpleasant, painful and distressing
condition for the woman. Such a physical condition would

take its toll in other areas. Constitutionally, the woman would have been weak, lacking iron. And psychologically, such a condition would have had a devastating effect on the woman's emotional life.

One might object that in today's society, she would at least have had recourse to medicine. But we would be wrong to assume that this was a society totally without medicine. The fact that this woman had spent good money on physicians suggests that she had every reason to suppose that these people had sufficient skills to cure her. Perhaps it would not be too high an order of speculation to suggest that she had witnessed others, with similar ailments, being healed by such physicians. There is no suggestion that the doctors who she saw were conmen. Perhaps desperation would indeed drive her to spend yet more money, but the context does not suggest fault lies with these doctors that this poor lady had, nonetheless, not been healed, but made worse. The reason would seem to be that her condition was not physical alone, but also spiritual, and she now had an appointment with the divine physician, who would heal her soul as well as her body. This was indeed a divine appointment.

Yet, humanly speaking, this encounter with Jesus appears to be accidental. She, of course, has every intention of pushing her way to Him.

Now, we must understand the extra danger and significance of her actions, in the times in which she lived.

Women, in their time of the month, were considered to be unclean. It was the Law that one should not touch a woman known to be in such a condition. That this woman had suffered in this way continuously for 12 years would make her extra specially aware of her own "uncleanness" before the Law, and, therefore, her insistence on touching Jesus' cloak is all the more remarkable. She would have known that her actions would, on a human level, make Jesus ceremonially unclean. Yet Jesus is the Lord God, and cannot be unclean, because He had given the very same Law, which many would have assumed would condemn this same woman. Therefore, her actions demonstrate a considerable faith on her part. There are those who would assume that her faith was simply in a man of magical-type miracles - something of a realistic conjurer, one might say. We have discussed above that Jesus was not a conjurer - He was and is the real deal. It is my contention that this woman had more than a faith, which is the result of the evidence of the miraculous. If it was merely the miraculous that she sought, then she would have interrupted Jesus, as others had done. Instead, she insists to herself "If only I may touch His clothes, I shall be made well". She knew she would be made well, because she knew that Jesus was not just a man or miracles, but of authority. She recognized that His actions occurred because He was God.

So, when Jesus asked "Who touched me?", the whole account of her faith became public. Jesus knew that power had gone from Him. So why did He ask a question? Why does God ever ask us questions? The answer to the question is not for the benefit of God. Jesus knew what had occurred. This appointment was not as accidental as it appeared. If the question was not for Jesus' benefit, who had access to other means of knowing the answer, then the question must have been for the benefit of the woman, and, by extension, for our benefit also. It enabled Jesus to be able to point out to the woman that her healing was not because of a mystical power associated with His cloak, but because of His divine authority. This is why he said to her "Daughter, your faith has made you well. Go in peace, and be healed of your affliction". Once again, the miracle is for a reason. The miracle is because of faith, and because of the power and authority of Jesus. The miracle did not occur to prove that Jesus was God. Jesus was no less God in the areas where He performed few or no miracles. The miracles are, rather, the corollary of the fact that He is God. It is very important to make this distinction, about the purpose of Jesus' miracles.

Jairus and His Daughter

At last we get to the main object lesson of this chapter, and, in so doing, you will see why I had to lay so much ground work with the accounts of the Gaderene man and the sick woman.

I think we need to make some positive comments about Jairus, before we even begin. That he ever came to Jesus in the first place was an act of bravery. Look at the manner of his entreaty.

And behold, one of the rulers of the synagogue came, Jairus by name. And when he saw Him, he fell at His feet.[4]

One of the things I like about the New King James Version (and, for that matter, the World English Bible too) is its retention of the word "behold", which we find in the Greek (admittedly only in Textus Receptus) as the little word ιδου. One preacher that I heard (I can't give a reference, as I can't remember his name) suggested that the word "behold" would really be best translated by a fanfare on a trumpet. So why do we have a fanfare here? Why is it such an important announcement, that one of the rulers of the synagogue would come to Jesus. It is because, as such an important man in the synagogue, Jairus had a lot to lose, by coming to Jesus. And not only did Jairus seek Jesus out, but he fell at His feet - an act of obeisance, at the very least, if not an act of worship. There must have been a modicum of faith in Jairus for him to make such a scene, in front of people who knew him, and would, perhaps, have tut-tutted that a ruler of their synagogue should have humiliated himself in such a way before this traveling rabbi.

Of course, Jairus had a motivation. But even his motivation was good. "My little daughter lies at the point of death". Jairus loved his little girl. Even if he might not have humiliated himself for his own benefit, he would do it for his little girl. And this is in a society that valued women a good deal less than our present society, and little girls even less than that. I am quite sure that there were other fathers who loved their daughters, but it is still worth emphasizing that Jairus was one such father. Even if his act of self-humiliation owed less to faith and more to love for his little girl, that can still only really be taken as a positive motivation on the part of this worried dad. And there were possibly other people, who Jairus could have turned to in need. That he came to Jesus does indeed speak of at least a measure of faith, as he declares "Come and lay Your hands on her, that she may be healed, and she will live." It must have taken Jairus a lot of guts to do what he just did. He is going against every convention of his position in society, to debase himself before this strange rabbi, because he has a measure of faith that this man might be the Messiah, and because of his love for his child. If you are a father (or a mother) then try to imagine the emotions going through this dear man's heart, as he makes his plea to Jesus. How his heart must have leapt, with the faint glimmerings of hope, when Jesus agreed to go with him, and this large crowd came along for the experience.

And then...

There is this woman. I had to comment on her story first, because at this point, I want to see this miracle through the eyes of Jairus, who was watching. The procession had stopped. Jesus is asking something about someone having touched Him. What could this mean? One thing it certainly meant! Jesus did not seem to share the same sense of urgency that Jairus had. It was not that this man had no compassion. But, if your little girl lay at home dying, would you not object a little to the time taken by Jesus for this woman, who, while certainly being sick, and certainly being justified in needing some of the Savior's time, was not actually dying at the moment. Not like his daughter! Couldn't Jesus have suggested she join the procession, and then heal her after his daughter? My little girl is in urgent need!

Yes, I know it is dangerous to make theology out of such suppositions, and reading between the lines. Those would have been my thoughts and feelings, however.

So, it might have been with a renewed sense of anxiety that Jairus noticed the procession move on again towards his house. Perhaps, what he dreaded most, was not really a surprise to him, as some of his household came to tell him "Your daughter is dead." But notice their follow-up statement "Why trouble the Teacher any further?" Why indeed? Perhaps Jesus' next words suggest that Jairus was of the same mind as his household. What was the point of going on now? How much faith did Jairus have? He has enough faith to go to the Man. He had enough faith to overcome his pride, and to humble himself. He had sufficient faith to believe that Jesus could heal his daughter. But he did not have the faith to believe that Jesus could raise the dead. Hope died with the death of the little girl.

Before we criticize Jairus, let's stand again in his sandals. How many of us have prayed for a some miracle in our lives, praying that we know that God **can** do this; we just don't know if it He **wants** to do it. This limit to our faith is what was experienced by Mary at the graveside of her brother. Was it a reproach when she declared "Lord, if You had been here, my brother would not have died."?[5] At least her sister Martha, who had said much the same thing, had added "But even now I know that whatever You ask of God, God will give You." How far does our faith go? How deep is it? To what extent does it come even close to matching the width, length, depth and height of the love of Christ - a love which we are told is the root and ground of faith?[6]

At this depth of hopelessness and despair, Jairus hears the words which are the whole purpose of what I want to underline in this chapter.

Do not be afraid; only believe.[7]

Luke reports a further phrase, so Jesus is giving an all-important 12-word 3-point sermon.
1. Do not be afraid.
2. Only believe.
3. And she will be made well.

Point one is that Jesus tells Jairus not to be afraid. This is a command. Of course, Jesus gives Jairus reasons for not being afraid, but those reasons are not what one might think. Jairus is having a crisis in his emotions. This could well be the biggest disaster ever to afflict his family. It is certainly in order to try to prevent this very occurrence that Jairus has been prepared to undergo humiliation, because of his love for his little girl. Now that effort has come to nothing. What effort can we possibly make to connect with God? Jesus is very clear on that. It is not our effort that connects us with our Heavenly Father. He commands us not to be afraid.

For what reason should Jairus not be afraid? What evidence could Jesus possibly provide, that would help Jairus in his moment of need?

Perhaps some of us, wedded to evidential apologetics, would suggest some possible evidences that Jesus could use.

1. Jesus could remind Jairus that he was capable of healing a woman, who had had severe bleeding for 12 years. After all, Jairus had just been a witness to that miracle. But I have just made clear that the purpose of the miracle was not to provide evidence. Besides, Jairus had almost certainly heard of other miracles. That is probably what had already drawn him to Jesus.

2. Were there any others who had been brought back to life at this point? I have already mentioned Lazarus, but that

event probably occurred after the healing of Jairus's daughter.

3. Jesus could have quoted Scripture at Jairus. He could have reminded him that both the prophets Elijah and Elisha had been involved in raising children from the dead.[8] Obviously, it is important to take people to Scripture. But even Scripture is not there to be used as a list of evidences, except in the sense that they confirm what we expect, because of our presupposition of the authority and power of God, based on what we have learned about that very subject from Scripture.

4. Jesus could have used logic. After all, this is much beloved by many apologists today. The logic might have been similar to that used by Abraham, when he was about to sacrifice his son, Isaac in Genesis 22. God had commanded Abraham to sacrifice his son Isaac. But God had already promised that Abraham's descendents would be reckoned through Isaac; Abraham had already believed that promise, and his faith had been credited to him as righteousness.[9] The only way that God's promise could still be true, if Abraham were to obey God and kill Isaac, is if God would raise him from the dead - and the book of Hebrews tells us that that is precisely the logic that Abraham used.[10] However, those who would use this as a justification for

secular logic forget one important fact. Abraham's logic was under the inspiration of the Holy Spirit, which is why the account is told in Genesis 22, and commented upon in Hebrews 11.

So, Jesus does not offer evidence to Jairus, in order to convince him how to obey his command not to be afraid. He does not offer the evidence that Jairus had seen with his own eyes, nor that which he had previously heard, nor that which he had read, nor that which he could work out by logic. What was Jesus' reason to Jairus for not being afraid. Just this.

ONLY BELIEVE

That's it. In a nutshell. Those two words constitute a command and an apologetic. Now we understand that these two words are not in a vacuum. Jairus is a man who believes in God. He knows of the nature of God. He knows the Scriptures. He is, after all, a ruler in the synagogue. In that context, and in the context of Jairus's anxiety, Jesus' words must be sufficient, because they are the words of authority. We have already learned that the reason for the miracles is to illustrate the divine authority of Jesus; that He was and is God. And that, therefore, is all the "evidence" that Jairus needs. And that is all the "evidence" we need. Because of who Jesus is, because of His very nature, He commands "Only believe". Just to be clear on this point, the Greek also has just two words, regardless of which Greek text we read.

μονον πιστευε

μονον - *monon* only, merely, just

πιστευε - *pisteue* believe

There can be no doubt, therefore, that these two words, only these two words, and exactly these two words, are what is needed in Jesus' 3-part sermon. The command to believe would not be sufficient, because it could be "believe and..." or "believe, even so..." or "believe, in spite of what you see and feel". Jesus' sermon has reached its main point, and it is not only "to believe" - it is "to only believe". There is nothing else necessary at this juncture than to believe. Faith is everything.

Of course, we must not take this out of context. I am not making a statement about the Gospel at this point. I am not suggesting an easy-believism as the answer to how we profess conversion. Jesus is not preaching the Gospel here. When He does so, He refers to repentance. Jesus is talking about the active participation of Jairus in the works of God. He is presenting Jairus with an apologetic. That apologetic involves no evidence, because no evidence is required, nor would it be appropriate. This is entirely a presuppositional apologetic. Of all the evidence that could have been presented, none has been offered. That is because Jairus knows who God is, and what He is like. This account is in the context of everything that Jairus has seen and known. Jairus, we must assume, knows where Jesus has been, prior to this meeting, because the Gaderene man had been around, pretty much stating that Jesus is God. Jairus, on this basis, has come to Jesus, thus humiliating himself. And not only has Jairus heard about the authority and nature of who Jesus is, he has witnessed this for himself, not as evidence (because in his distress, the evidence had failed to convince him), but as an essential statement of the power and authority vested in Jesus, the Son of the Most High God. Which discussion brings us to the third point of Jesus' 12-word sermon - the application.

She will be made well.

Does Jairus have the proof that his little daughter will be made well? Yes, he does, if he analyses that proof properly, because it is not proven by evidence. Evidence, after all, proves nothing. Evidence is only relevant, when it is interpreted by a person's worldview - their presupposition. If Jairus relied on evidence alone at this point, he would be like those of us who pray "I know you **can** do this, God - I just don't know whether you **want** to do this for me." Jairus's belief is not to be because the evidence, but because of the person - because of his presupposition.

Did Jairus believe at this point? I cannot prove that he did, but I strongly suspect that, in fact, he did. After all, when Jesus got to the house, the mourners stopped their mourning long enough to mock Jesus and laugh at him for His words. Yet Jairus accepted Jesus into his home, and Jesus took him and his wife into the place where the child lay. And the miracle He performed was one of complete and utter divine authority. He commanded the dead girl to rise, and she did.

Conclusion

As I have stated several times, there is so much more that I could draw out of this passage. Yet I think that this lesson will suffice. My purpose has been to show the context of Jesus' works, which illustrate, not prove, his authority. In other words, we do not believe in the authority of Jesus, because of the miracles. Rather, we believe in the authority of Jesus, and therefore the miracles make sense. That is why we have had to make such a detailed analysis of how this whole passage works as an apologetic, climaxing in those two powerful words - Only Believe. Those are the words that we carry forward to the rest of the book, and they are the foundation upon which all the other things that I say will be built. We are to believe, but that statement is insufficient. Jesus says that we are to "Only believe". You already have all the evidence you need - Only believe. Interpret the evidence according to that belief. Remember who God is, and study His nature (as we have done here with the nature of the Second Person of God the Trinity).

That is all the proof we need for the bedrock of our faith. Everything else is built on that foundation. If it were not so, then Jesus would have offered Jairus a multitude of proofs. As we study other parts of the Bible, we will see the relevance of Jesus' main sermon point to Jairus, and it is worth repeating again and again. Only believe. Only **believe. Only** believe.

---

[1] See, for example, the Wikipedia article about this show, < https://en.wikipedia.org/wiki/Messiah_%28Derren_Brown_s pecial%29 >, retrieved 1/2/2016

[2] See, for example, Exodus 7:22

[3] Mark 5:18-20

[4] Mark 5:22

[5] John 11:1-45

[6] Ephesians 3:17-18

[7] Mark 5:36

[8] 1 Kings 17:22 and 2 Kings 4:34-35

[9] Genesis 15:6

[10] Hebrews 11:19

03 Prove that God Exists

It is reasonable, is it not, for the atheist to demand that we prove the existence of God. After all, if God exists, there should surely be empirical proof that He exists. So this sort of challenge to the Christian is a common challenge. "Why should I believe something that can't be proved?"

The problem with the above challenges is that they are based on faulty assumptions. We have already discussed in chapter 1 how there are certain questions that do not deserve an answer, with respect to the paradigm of the question. Just to repeat our example given there; there is no answer to the question "Have you stopped beating your wife yet?" within the paradigm of the question, because any answer given accepts the question's presupposition that there was once a time when you did beat your wife. In the same way, the questions above are not as neutral as they might at first appear.

For that reason, this chapter will challenge the popular notion that it is reasonable for the atheist to demand evidence that proves the existence of God. Such "proof", after all, is predicated on a partial definition of the word "proof". Moreover, the request for "empirical" proof assumes that such empiricism exists.

The Christian is often left floundering, not knowing how to respond to common attacks or questions from atheists. A little study of apologetics goes a long way, and those who delve into this subject are often surprised to find how weak the arguments against God are. Here are just five common old chestnuts, thrown at the believer.

- You have faith, but I have reason.

- You have faith, but I have science.

- Why should the god of Christianity be the only one which is real? Other religions have holy books, which claim that their way is correct.

- As a Christian, you do not believe in all the other gods. As an atheist, I just believe in one god less than you.

- I don't like how God is described in the Bible, so, since he is so unpleasant, he obviously doesn't exist.

The last of these arguments against God was put succinctly by Richard Dawkins in his atheist manifesto, *The God Delusion*.

The God of the Old Testament is arguably the most unpleasant character in all fiction: jealous and proud of it; a petty, unjust, unforgiving control-freak; a vindictive, bloodthirsty ethnic cleanser; a misogynistic, homophobic, racist, infanticidal, genocidal, filicidal, pestilential, megalomaniacal, sadomasochistic, capriciously malevolent bully. Those of us schooled from infancy in his ways can become desensitized to their horror.[1]

Illogical Arguments Against God

It has been a constant source of surprise to me, that those atheists, who claim to be led by reason alone, will use such illogical arguments against God. Indeed, I developed an entire talk, teaching how classical logical fallacies work, illustrating every fallacy type from *The God Delusion*.[2] The basic points of that talk are included in an appendix to this book.

The lack of logic of such atheists was exemplified for me in an experience on the Internet about 15 years ago. Those ancient days of the Internet, at the turn of the century, were before the days of Twitter and Facebook. There were, however, a number of Internet forums for discussion. I had joined one of these. An atheist contributor insisted that there was no god, because the Bible was full of contradictions. I challenged him to describe just one. These days, if I make such a challenge, I actually allow for three "contradictions", but I also state that if the questioner asks more than three, I will simply answer the first three and ignore the rest. However, I was more naïve in those days. So this atheist posted a list of 33 alleged contradictions. I spent an entire day, working through these "contradictions", and answered every single one, in detail. In less than five minutes after I had posted my responses, the atheist returned with the comment that my arguments were all rubbish; at least that was the gist of what he said. At that point, I did what I should have done in the first place. I copied a section of one of his questions, and pasted it into a search engine. I soon discovered that his entire list of objections had been copied and pasted from an atheist website. He had done zero research, and had paid zero attention to anything that I had written.

Biblical Logic

In the face of such appalling logic, it will be instructive to examine some biblical logic. Arguably, the most logical character in the New Testament, after Jesus Himself, would be the apostle Paul. A brilliant man, the foundational work of his ideas must surely be his epistle to the Romans, which is not just the longest letter in the New Testament, it is the longest surviving letter of any sort from the ancient world. Surely, the foundational ideas of Romans are contained in chapter 1. There are 10 verses in particular, to which I wish to draw your attention.

> 16. *For I am not ashamed of the gospel of Christ, for it is the power of God to salvation for everyone who believes, for the Jew first and also for the Greek. 17. For in it the righteousness of God is revealed from faith to faith; as it is written, "THE JUST SHALL LIVE BY FAITH." 18. For the wrath of God is revealed from heaven against all ungodliness*

and unrighteousness of men, who suppress the truth in unrighteousness, 19. because what may be known of God is manifest in them, for God has shown it to them. 20. For since the creation of the world His invisible attributes are clearly seen, being understood by the things that are made, even His eternal power and Godhead, so that they are without excuse, 21. because, although they knew God, they did not glorify Him as God, nor were thankful, but became futile in their thoughts, and their foolish hearts were darkened. 22. Professing to be wise, they became fools, 23. and changed the glory of the incorruptible God into an image made like corruptible man—and birds and four-footed animals and creeping things. 24. Therefore God also gave them up to uncleanness, in the lusts of their hearts, to dishonor their bodies among themselves, 25. who exchanged the truth of God for the lie, and worshiped and served the creature rather than the Creator, who is blessed forever. Amen.[3]

It is important to note that this great intellectual was not ashamed of the Gospel. There have been so many times in my life when I have been ashamed of the Gospel. Surely, I have thought, this person will think I am less than sound, if I admit that I believe these wonderful truths. The apostle makes it clear that this should never be our position. The Gospel is for everyone. Not that everyone will be saved, but certainly that all sorts of people will be saved, because the Gospel is available for everyone who believes.

Having started this section with what some might think is an unintellectual comment, the apostle goes on to lay down an impeccable framework of logic. He turns from those who believe, to those who do not believe. Just as the Gospel is for all kinds of people, so the ones who do not believe come from every walk of life, and every nationality and people group. With characteristic boldness, Paul declares that the wrath of god is revealed on such people.

The Pious Heathen

Well, that is a bit unfair, isn't it? This objection is voiced, not just by unbelievers, but also by many who own the name Christian. Indeed, this argument leads to yet another atheist objection to the existence of God to add to those above.

- What about those people who have never heard about Jesus?

This objection is also voiced by many within the church. If someone has never had the chance of hearing about Jesus, surely God will not condemn them to hell. Surely it would be unfair of God to send someone to hell, because they don't believe in Jesus, especially if they haven't heard.

Yet this objection, like the others above, is logically fallacious, and I will endeavor to show you why.

Those who know me will know that I have a great fondness for C.S. Lewis and his writings. Yet Lewis got this point wrong. In the last of his wonderful Chronicles of Narnia, *The Last Battle*[4], there is a just soldier called Emeth from Calormen - the nation which has invaded and conquered Narnia. Having entered into the stable, he does not realize that he has died, and that the place he is now searching is actually Aslan's country. As a devout Calormene, he has spent his life worshiping the vile demonic god Tash. Expecting to meet Tash, he instead encounters Aslan. For political reasons, some of the Calormene leaders (and Narnian renegades) had been putting it about that Aslan and Tash were one and the same, and referred to him/it as Tashlan. So, meeting Aslan, Emeth asks if it is true that he and Tash are the same. Aslan tells him "No", but states that "all the service thou hast done to Tash, I accept as service done to me". He tells him that Emeth's devotion to Tash was really devotion to Aslan. This doctrine is beginning to crop up frequently among so-called evangelicals. It is the concept of the pious heathen, whose service to his pagan god is actually, unknown to him, service to Jesus. This argument provides some people with a degree of comfort. But it is a false comfort, and it is vital that we see that this argument, too, is fallacious.

A first argument against the pious heathen can appeal to a simple logic. Suppose it were true that the pious heathen, who has never heard about Jesus, goes to heaven when he dies, because Jesus accepts the service done to his pagan deity as service to him. Why, then, do we send missionaries to such people? If Fred has spent his life in ignorance, blindly worshiping a false god, and being a good man, but then hears about Jesus from the missionary, what is the change in his status now? If he refuses to accept this Gospel, he has now embarked on the road to hell. Yet, just a few hours before, when he had not met this missionary, he was on the road to heaven, as a pious heathen! In other words, the preaching of the Gospel by this missionary has actually removed salvation from Fred. I mean this next point literally - why in the name of all that is holy would we ever want to do such a thing? Surely, it is a great injustice, then, to preach the Gospel to any new tribe. It would be better to build huge walls around the places where Christian missionaries have not yet been, to prevent these people ever hearing about the Jesus, whose message condemns otherwise righteous people to hell.

And yet, Jesus commanded us to preach the Gospel to all the world. Why would He do this? Do you honestly believe Jesus would have given us such a command, if the outworking of this command were so tragic?

The truth is the opposite. These unevangelized people would actually go to hell, if they did not hear the Gospel.

But, but but???

To understand this point better, we need to continue with Romans 1.

What may be known of God is manifest in them, for God has shown it to them. For since the creation of the world His invisible attributes are clearly seen, being understood by the things that are made, even His eternal power and Godhead, so that they are without excuse.

Read the first sentence above carefully. It tells us that everybody already knows about God. Everything about God that is necessary for them to know has already been shown to them, to their condemnation. The information that they still need is the Gospel, which is the power of God unto salvation.

How can this be?

General Revelation

The next sentence tells us that God's invisible attributes are clearly seen. Where are they seen, if these people do not have a Bible? His attributes are seen in creation. "The heavens declare the glory of God", reminds the psalmist in Psalm 19:1. God's revelation of Himself is in two parts.

- Special Revelation, in the Bible.
- General Revelation, in the whole of creation.

What can we learn about God from His creation? We learn that He is the Almighty Creator. For reasons still to be discussed, God's existence is self-evident throughout creation. "Even his eternal power and Godhead" are seen through creation. Not only can we understand about the nature of God, we can also understand that we have disobeyed this Almighty Creator. In the next chapter of Romans, Paul explains that Gentiles - and he is using the term generally to describe unbelievers - "show the work of the law written in their hearts, their conscience also bearing witness, and between themselves their thoughts accusing or else excusing them".[5] God has given each of us a conscience. This conscience is badly damaged in many people, but it still has remnants of honesty from God. It is this conscience that helps people to understand that there is right and wrong - and the illogicality of the atheists' attempts to define right and wrong are discussed later. Back in Romans 1, Paul reminds us that such people already know right from wrong, but they "suppress the truth in unrighteousness".

General revelation, therefore, gives people a certain amount of knowledge of God. It enables them to know, not just that there is **a** god, but that **the** God is the God of the Bible, but, in addition, it gives them to know that they are sinners against this God, having broken what remnant of the Law of God remains unsuppressed in their conscience. Therefore, general revelation gives enough knowledge justifiably to condemn the so-called pious heathen and the atheist alike. The knowledge given is insufficient for salvation. The knowledge of salvation requires the preaching of the Gospel.

The soft-hearted (and I honestly do not mean that term as an insult) would still object that God seems unfair, if these people are condemned for not having the Gospel. Yet the Bible helps us to understand this, by reminding us of the Sovereignty of God. God does not make mistakes. It is my belief - and I will back this up - that if a so-called pious heathen would have received the Gospel and repented, had he heard it, then God would have made sure that he did indeed hear it, by sending a suitable missionary.

I can produce a couple of examples to back this point up. In Acts 10, we read about a centurion called Cornelius. We are told that he was a devout man who feared God. Yet, he had not heard the Gospel. While not putting such thoughts exactly into words, he must have been trying in his own way to find out who this unknown God was, and what He was like. God heard that prayer, and, to cut a long story short, He prepared Peter, and then sent him to Cornelius. The result of this was that Cornelius and his family were saved. The Scripture makes clear that this was not a chance encounter. God planned how He would save this Gentile family, and that the event would also serve as an education for the apostle Peter. I honestly believe that the same sort of thing can happen today, and I have heard of numerous anecdotes from missionaries, who find the reception of the Gospel they preach to be easier than they expected, because, for some reason, the people to who they are speaking have already been searching for this true God, and the arrival of the missionary is the answer to their prayer.

The other side of the coin, however, must also be made. The passage from Romans 1 quoted above makes it very clear that there is actually no such thing as an atheist. An atheist is someone who says that they do not believe in God. Yet, Romans 1 makes clear that these people indeed know God, but fail to acknowledge Him. The reason why they fail to acknowledge Him is sobering. It is because they prefer their sin. We need to examine this point more closely, and we will start by repeating Romans 1:20.

> *For since the creation of the world His invisible attributes are clearly seen, being understood by the things that are made, even His eternal power and Godhead, so that they are without excuse.*

We have not yet noted the final phrase. These unbelievers are "without excuse". A friend of mine has frequently commented thus: No one is sent to hell, because they don't know God. They are sent to hell, for failing to acknowledge the God, who they know exists. Ray Comfort has given an apt title to one of his books about evangelism; "God Does Not Believe in Atheists". Not only does God not believe in atheists, nether should we.

Romans 1:21 continues thus:

Although they knew God, they did not glorify Him as God,
nor were thankful, but became futile in their thoughts, and
their foolish hearts were darkened.

"Although they knew God..." The apostle makes clear that the problem these people have is not due to ignorance. No one dies of ignorance. It is again emphasized that everyone knows God, in the sense that they know He exists, and have a measure of knowledge of what He is like, such as his eternal power and Godhead. Their failure was not one of ignorance, it was one of foolishness. In their foolishness, they "did not glorify Him as God." The verse describes them as "foolish".

Intellectual Fools

Now there are some atheists who are very clever. Indeed, there are many highly intellectual atheists, who know things that I didn't even know existed, who can speak multiple languages, and understand deep principles of math or physics. But when the Bible describes someone as foolish, it is not making a comment about their intelligence - it is making a comment about their moral responsibility.

At the beginning of his film about apologetics, *How to Answer the Fool*, apologist Sye ten Bruggencate gives an example of someone who does not believe in words. He comments that if someone said that they did not believe in words, we would not believe them, because we and they would see that they were using words to make their argument. Nor would we respect them. We would certainly not waste any time trying to prove to them that words actually exist. Indeed, we would consider them foolish.

This passage in Romans has made clear that everyone actually knows that God exists. Moreover, the passage shows that every piece of evidence necessary to prove to them that God exists, and has a demand on their lives, not only already exists, but is already known by them. And it goes on to say that those who do not acknowledge God are foolish. What further evidence do these people need to convince them that God exists? None. How many people actually require proof that God exists? None. So why do Christians seem to spend so much time providing evidence to the non-Christian that God exists? Christian bookstores are replete with titles that describe evidence for this, that or the other. My own normal field of expertise - creationism - is one of the worst offenders. We expend huge quantities of intellectual energy, providing evidence that will, we hope, refute the theory of evolution, and point people to the truth of creation, forgetting that, if we only convert them to creation, without presenting them with the Gospel, then they are still going to hell. On the other side of the coin are innumerable apologists - let's call them evidential apologists - who don't care about the truth of Genesis, and think that you can believe what you like on that subject, so long as they can present neutral evidence that will establish the existence of God. When we start our defense of the faith from the Bible, we see that there is, in fact, no such thing as neutral evidence, and the search to convince people by such methods is as futile as the unbelievers' refusal to glorify God as God.

Having introduced the concept of apologists, who attempt to defend the faith in a way that I would describe as erroneous, I will need to examine their arguments and methodologies. But not yet! That can wait for a later chapter. The principle, which I need to underline at the moment is that the Bible maintains that the existence of God, and His nature, is self-evident, and does not require "neutral" proof. Indeed, I will go on to show that neutral proof does not exist. As there is no need to prove the existence of God, we can start our defense of the faith by assuming that God exists. This is our *presupposition*. A presupposition is our starting point. It is what we believe, before we even commence the argument. In order to justify this position further, I will need to show you two corollaries of the presupposition that God exists.

- That those who do not presuppose the existence of God are not neutral. They have their own presupposition.
- The presupposition that God either does not exist, or is not actively in control, is illogical.

The Bible makes both of these points very clear, and we will examine these points from Scripture. Indeed, we should add to our presupposition that, not only does God exist, but He is the

God of the Bible, and not any other God, and that the Bible is true. Again, I will demonstrate that the opposite presupposition is illogical, and leads, inevitably, to fallacies that we can justifiably label as foolish, just as the Bible does.

Professing to be wise, they became fools, and changed the glory of the incorruptible God into an image made like corruptible man—and birds and four-footed animals and creeping things.

How fair is this as a criticism of today's atheist? Surely, they are more sophisticated that the pagans of old. They do not carve idols out of wood to worship. Yet, greater sophistication does not imply greater wisdom. Once again, we must note that wisdom does not equate to intelligence. These people, then, profess to be wise, but they are not. Any concept of "creation", in its broadest possible interpretation, is, in fact, an image. Just because that image exists in their intellect, rather than as a wooden carving, does not make it any the less an image. Of course, you might argue that they do not create images of animals. Yet, in a sense that is precisely what the evolutionist is doing, maintaining that "creation" occurs by the gradual evolution of complex animals from simpler ones. They consider the driving force for nature to be nature itself, rather than God. They are not glorifying God as God - and, in that criticism, one has to include many Christians, who believe they can marry their belief in the Bible with a belief in evolution. It is for these reasons that we assert that such people are worshiping and serving the creature rather than the Creator. The apostle Paul is very strong in his condemnation of this intellectual position. He does not mince his words. He describes it, not merely as a lie, but as *The Lie*.

---

[1] Dawkins, Richard (2008). *The God Delusion* (p. 51). Houghton Mifflin Harcourt. Kindle Edition.

[2] Taylor, Paul (2013), *Deconstructing Dawkins*, (Creation Today video download)

[3] Romans 1:16-25

[4] Lewis, C.S (2008), *The Last Battle*, (HarperCollins reprint edition)

[5] Romans 2:15

04 The Beginning of Wisdom

Many of the words associated with the intellect are incorrectly used in everyday speech. Examples of these include wisdom, knowledge, ignorance and foolishness.

For many people, the word ignorant is an insult. It is frequently used in such a manner. However, when considered carefully, we will realize that a sentence in which someone is accused of ignorance usually implies that the culprit is ignorant of something specific. For example, consider the following.

"He refused to stand up to let the pregnant lady sit down."

"Well, he's just ignorant."

In this example, the word ignorant is being used as an insult, but the second voice's sentence is not really complete. He / she could more fully have said "Well, he's just ignorant of good manners."

In fact, ignorance is not necessarily an insult. An American friend of mine, when in Britain, used a word, which is considered completely appropriate in the US, but is considered mildly rude in Britain. (Clue: it rhymes with "summer", but begins with "b"). However, he was not being rude. In the proper sense of the word, he was ignorant. That did not mean he was unintelligent. Nor did it mean he was actually rude, and, as a point of fact, this particular friend went to enormous lengths to fit in with the culture of the people around him - an example that I have tried to follow in reverse , as I now live in America. (There are, after all, words and mannerisms that British people use happily, which are considered rude in America).

Therefore, the word ignorance is the opposite of the word knowledge. Sometimes people use the word ignorant as if it is the opposite of wisdom. It is not. The opposite of wisdom is foolishness. This chapter is about wisdom, and, therefore, it is also about foolishness.

Wisdom in the Bible

Proverbs 9:10 states:

> *The fear of the LORD is the beginning of wisdom, And the knowledge of the Holy One is understanding.*

Proverbs is a poetic book, and Hebrew poetry is recognizable in English. Like much English poetry, it frequently consists of couplets, but unlike English couplets, the lines do not rhyme. Instead they contain similar or complementary ideas. It is like a rhyming of thought, rather than a rhyming of sound. So, the couplet of ideas is as follows:

> *The fear of the LORD is the beginning of wisdom,*

> *And the knowledge of the Holy One is understanding.*

This couplet contains ideas which are similar, but also contrasted. Wisdom is contrasted with knowledge, yet true knowledge is shown to be linked to understanding. However, the root of the wisdom is the fear of the Lord. Books and chapters have been written about the use of the word "fear" in "fear of the Lord". Some commentators like to minimize the concept of fear. While it is true that God is not actually expecting us to be "afraid", in the sense of being in abject terror, nevertheless the word implies a high level of reverence. We are not to approach God as if He is our mate, our chum, our buddy, as some preachers seem to imply. He is not that. He is a loving father, but He is altogether other, and altogether royal, and, as this passage insists, He is altogether holy. If we are in sin, then we should most definitely be in fear, even in our modern understanding of that word. But even when we approach Him as our Heavenly Father, coming into His loving presence through the merit of our Savior Jesus Christ, we are still not to do so flippantly, or casually. He is our Father, and He is also the Lord of the Universe.

The first line of the Proverbs 9:10 couplet tells us that this fear of the Lord is the beginning of wisdom. Therefore, there is no wisdom without the fear of the Lord.

Now, wisdom is not the same as knowledge. Let's not push the distinction too far, because many of you will know (and we will check this in the next chapter) that Proverbs also tells us that the fear of the Lord is the beginning of knowledge. However, as we are concentrating on wisdom, let's be clear that wisdom is not knowledge, and therefore foolishness is not ignorance. It is clear, then, that it is possible to be wise, whole being ignorant, and also foolish, while having much knowledge. For example:

The ear of the wise seeks knowledge.[1]

The person being described in this verse is, in a sense, ignorant. Obviously, he is aware that he is ignorant, and, therefore, he seeks knowledge. But he does not yet have that knowledge, so is, to that extent, ignorant of the knowledge that he is going to attain. Very soon he will be considerably less ignorant, but the acquisition of knowledge will take time, and will require the use of his attention - in this case, by his listening with his ear. However, he is already wise. Although he does not yet have the knowledge, which he will soon attain, he is already wise, because he has the sense to know his ignorance, and to do something about it.

A young preacher may not yet know all the arts of exegesis. But he is already wise if he seeks out the company of a more learned and senior preacher, to be his mentor. A young wife, with little experience or understanding of how to be a new mother, is already wise, if she calls on a senior Christian lady, to train her. This same truth applies to all walks of life.

Conversely, the young husband, who frequently lays down the law on how children should be raised, and is a vocal "expert" on child-rearing, before ever becoming a father, is probably behaving foolishly.

The Bible maintains that there is no true wisdom without the fear of the Lord. That is why, in the previous chapter, we saw from Romans 1 that everyone actually knows God exists, but that there are some who refuse to glorify Him as God, and therefore these people are fools, however much knowledge they may possess.

The Biblical Fool

The Bible reminds us of this important principle.

> *The fool has said in his heart, "There is no God."* [2]

Remember that a fool is someone who lacks wisdom, not someone who lacks knowledge. Therefore, the person who states that there is no God might have a great deal of knowledge, and might be one of the cleverest people on earth. They might be able to win a debate hands down against the likes of me. Yet, the Bible says that this person is a fool. They cannot even begin the journey into wisdom, because they have no fear of the Lord. Dr. Greg Bahnsen puts it thus:

> *The Christian cannot forever be defensively constructing atomistic answers to the endless variety of unbelieving*

*criticisms; he must take the offensive and show the
unbeliever that he has no intelligible place to stand, no
consistent epistemology, no justification for meaningful
discourse, predication, or argumentation. The pseudo-
wisdom of the world must be reduced to foolishness—in which
case none of the unbeliever's criticisms have any force. If we
are to understand how to answer the fool, if we are to be able
to demonstrate that God has made the pseudo-wisdom of the
world foolish, then we must first study the biblical conception
of the fool and his foolishness.*[3]

Bahnsen proceeds to describe, from Proverbs, some of the
characteristics of a fool. Once again, we must emphasize that
the person being here described may well be highly intelligent.

*The fool has utter self-confidence and imagines himself to
be intellectually autonomous.*[4]

Proverbs 12:15 tells us that "The way of a fool is right in his
own eyes". Until the Holy Spirit opens the eyes of such a
person, they assume themselves to be right. Many has been
the time, when I have been having what might be termed an
apologetic conversation with an atheist, that they have even
lectured me on my wisdom, while all the time I have shown
them that their position is logically fallacious. Consider this
conversation from a Facebook thread.

Me: As an atheist, what do you actually know for sure, and how do you know it?

ND: The same way anybody can be said to "know". You are talking about epistemology (how we know what we know) on one hand and knowledge (a subset of belief) on the other. Complete certainty is impossible.

Me: Can you be completely certain that complete certainty is impossible? Can you not see that this is an illogical position to take?

ND: I know that I exist in some way, shape or form. I am an avid student of science.

Me: "I know that I exist in some way, shape of form." How do you know that?

ND: I do not waste my time debating presuppositional apologists. Tell me one thing you know for CERTAIN. The burden of proof is on you to demonstrate that complete certainty is attainable.

Me: If you want a logical proof that "certainty is possible", I have already provided it. The opposite statement is that "certainty is impossible". I have already shown that this is an illogical statement. Therefore, it is logical to state that "certainty is possible".

It is often difficult for an atheist to understand the illogicality of stating that "complete certainty is impossible". Their presuppositions do not give them a standard, against which to measure. Therefore, their tendency is to throw this argument back. This is a part of their biblical foolishness.

It was noteworthy that, in between the comments quoted above, another contributor, claiming to be a Christian, kept interjecting that I was being mean in the conversation.

DD: What about those of the Islamic tradition who believe that Allah has revealed the truth to them? They, no doubt, see us as having it wrong, just as we see them as having it wrong. We cannot fully grasp that universal truth. We just get as close as we can.

Me: Jesus said "I am the way, the truth, and the life. No one comes to the Father but by me". Jesus maintained that He was the ONLY way. Was he lying?

DD: Is every Muslim too stupid to understand the truth?

You will see that the inclusivist "Christian", DD, confused the concept of stupidity with foolishness, which is exactly where we began this chapter. Such inclusivist Christians can be frustrating, as they frequently, as in this case, take the moral "high ground" castigating the Christian for being intolerant, or unloving, or both. For now, it is probably more edifying to return to Scripture, and see what it says about the personification of wisdom.

Personification of Wisdom

Proverbs gives us a frequent personification of wisdom. Perhaps the most intriguing such passage is this:

"The LORD possessed me at the beginning of His way, Before His works of old. I have been established from everlasting, From the beginning, before there was ever an earth. When there were no depths I was brought forth, When there were no fountains abounding with water. Before the mountains were settled, Before the hills, I was brought forth; While as yet He had not made the earth or the fields, Or the primal dust of the world. When He prepared the heavens, I was there, When He drew a circle on the face of the deep, When He established the clouds above, When He strengthened the fountains of the deep, When He assigned to the sea its limit, So that the waters would not transgress His command, When He marked out the foundations of the earth, Then I was beside Him as a master craftsman; And I was daily His delight, Rejoicing always before Him, Rejoicing in His inhabited world, And my delight was with the sons of men. "Now therefore, listen to me, my children, For blessed are those who keep my ways. Hear instruction and be wise, And do not disdain it. Blessed is the man who listens to me, Watching daily at my gates, Waiting at the posts of my doors. For whoever finds me

finds life, And obtains favor from the LORD; But he who sins against me wrongs his own soul; All those who hate me love death."[5]

The personification of wisdom in Proverbs is female. We need not be too concerned about that. It is somewhat similar (though not exactly the same) as the way that many European languages (other than English) use gender for inanimate objects. If we ignore the gender issue attached to Wisdom, as a personification in Proverbs, we can see who is actually being described. Who was "at the beginning of [the LORD's] way, before His works of old"? Who was "beside Him as a master craftsman"? And of whom can it be said "whoever finds me finds life"? This seems to me to be one of the clearest Messianic passages of the Old Testament. Note the similarity of the last phrase that I quoted with the best known verse in the Bible, John 3:16.

For God so loved the world that He gave His only begotten Son, that whoever believes in Him should not perish but have everlasting life.

No analogy should be pushed too far. Yet, there does seem to be a link between the acquisition of wisdom and true faith in Jesus Christ. Jesus Himself seemed to make the same connection.

For John came neither eating nor drinking, and they say, 'He has a demon.' The Son of Man came eating and drinking, and they say, 'Look, a glutton and a winebibber, a friend of tax collectors and sinners!' But wisdom is justified by her children."[6]

John Gill, commenting on this verse, said the following:

Either the wisdom of God, in making use of ministers of a different disposition and deportment, whereby some are gained, and others left inexcusable: or the Gospel, in which there is such a display of divine wisdom, which is vindicated from the charge of licentiousness, by the agreeable lives and conversations of the children of God: or rather Christ himself, who is the wisdom of God; and in whom are hid all the treasures of wisdom and knowledge; who, however he may be traduced by ignorant and malicious men, yet will be acquitted from all such charges, as here insinuated, by all the true sons of wisdom; or by such, who are made wise unto salvation. We may learn from hence, that no sort of preachers and preaching will please some men; that the best of Gospel ministers may be reproached as libertines, or madmen; and that they will be sooner, or later, justified and cleared from all such aspersions.[7]

The obvious corollary of what we are saying is that wisdom involves the knowledge of a person. We have seen that wisdom and knowledge are not the same; that one can be wise, without having knowledge. This is because the actual knowledge that is required for wisdom is the knowledge of the person of Jesus Christ.

The fear of the LORD is the beginning of wisdom,

And the knowledge of the Holy One is understanding.

The French language separates these two different kinds of knowledge into two words; *savoir* and *connaître*. That is why the concept of wisdom is so closely bound with the subject of apologetics; the defence of the faith. We have much more to say on the subject of wisdom, but this chapter has been about "The Beginning of Wisdom".

---

[1] Proverbs 18:15

[2] Psalm 14:1

[3] Bahnsen, Greg (2011). **Always Ready:** Directions for Defending the Faith (Kindle Locations 927-934). (Covenant Media Press: Kindle Edition)

[4] *ibid*

[5] Proverbs 8:22-36

[6] Matthew 11:18-19

[7] Gill, John (2012-08-02). John Gill's Exposition of the Entire Bible (Kindle Locations 234984-234990). Kindle Edition.

05 The Beginning of Knowledge

We live in a low information society.

"Surely not!" I hear you cry. It is true that we seem to have access to more information than we have ever had. I don't know if Pub Quizzes in England have been affected by people trying to use their cellphones under the table to Google an answer, but the availability of information has not led to a greater knowledge of information among the populace.

Take the average Christian. A study by LifeWay in 2012 indicated that only 19% of Christians read their Bible every day.

When asked how often they personally (not as part of a church worship service) read the Bible, a similar number respond "Every Day" (19 percent) as respond "Rarely/Never" (18 percent). A quarter indicate they read the Bible a few times a week. Fourteen percent say they read the Bible "Once a Week" and another 22 percent say "Once a Month" or "A Few Times a Month."[1]

I have not found a survey telling us how many Christians have read the Bible all the way through. However, anecdotally, I would suggest that it is not many. This is despite the fact that the task is not onerous. If you read a chapter a day, for example, you will have read the Bible through in three years.

Try asking someone who has been a Christian 12 years if they have read the Bible through four times!

Was this always the case? No, it was not. Despite the rumors that people in Bible times were more primitive than we are, the impression I get is the reverse. I recognize that when the fisherman, Peter, began to preach in Acts 2, that he was being inspired by the Holy Spirit. Nevertheless, context suggests that the Scriptural background he used was something already familiar to him, and also familiar to his audience. This was a high information society, that knew the Scriptures - and they knew these things without the aid of smartphones. They knew them, because of the instructions of Scripture itself, which guidelines were published for people of all ranks and classes, if there should be such ranks and classes among God's people. One such instruction would be:

> "And these words which I command you today shall be in your heart. You shall teach them diligently to your children, and shall talk of them when you sit in your house, when you walk by the way, when you lie down, and when you rise up. You shall bind them as a sign on your hand, and they shall be as frontlets between your eyes. You shall write them on the doorposts of your house and on your gates.[2]

The things of God are to be taught from generation to generation. It is our responsibility as parents to make sure that this is the case. That God's people have not always fulfilled their part in this is witnessed by the following passage:

> So the people served the Lord all the days of Joshua, and all the days of the elders who outlived Joshua, who had seen all the great works of the Lord which He had done for Israel. Now Joshua the son of Nun, the servant of the Lord, died when he was one hundred and ten years old. And they buried him within the border of his inheritance at Timnath Heres, in the mountains of Ephraim, on the north side of Mount Gaash. When all that generation had been gathered to their fathers, another generation arose after them who did not know the Lord nor the work which He had done for Israel.[3]

Why did this new generation not know the Lord? It is probably because they had become a low information society. Their parents must not have obeyed what God had commanded in Deuteronomy 6:6-9.

Biblical Epistemology

Where does knowledge come from? The Bible and the world have entirely different answers to this question. As Christians, it surely ought to be the case that we adopt the biblical answer to the question, yet most famous Christian apologists use the world's answer. We will discuss the world's answer later. The biblical answer is to be found in Proverbs 1:7.

The fear of the LORD is the beginning of knowledge.

The previous chapter concentrated on the proverb that "the fear of the LORD is the beginning of wisdom". We spent quite a bit of effort showing that wisdom and knowledge are not the same thing. Yet it is clear that the starting point for both is the same - they start in our attitude to God. Since the fear of the Lord is the beginning of knowledge, we are saying it is the case that all knowledge has come from Him, and without Him, there is no knowledge.

"But", you might object "there are a lot of people who do not believe in God, who are often very clever; they have a lot of knowledge". This is true. We have, however, already seen that the Bible tells us that such people do really know that God exists, but they refuse to glorify Him as God. The fact that God exists is the explanation for their knowledge. All the vast knowledge that these clever people have is from God, and therefore they ought to worship Him, but they refuse to glorify Him as God.

The technical word for the study of how we know what we know is *epistemology*. The Bible is clear that we know what we know, because such knowledge has come from God. Now this is clearly a very different foundation from the foundation for epistemology used by the world. Van Til described biblical epistemology thus.

The central concern of a truly biblical apologetic method is... to show that without presupposing the Christian worldview, all of man's reasoning, experience, interpretation, etc., is unintelligible. Only the transcendent revelation of God can provide the philosophically necessary preconditions for logic, science, morality, etc., in which case those who oppose the faith are reduced to utter foolishness and intellectually have nowhere to stand in objecting to Christianity's truth-claims.[4]

In a nutshell, van Til is saying that knowledge is dependent on the presuppositions that

1. God exists (that is, the Triune God of the Bible)

2. The Bible is true

Secular Epistemology

In contrast with this quite simple definition of epistemology in the Bible, the secular definitions are complex and hard to understand. The article in the Encyclopaedia Britannica runs to 27 pages, when printed. The article, however, helpfully breaks up the types of knowledge into groups. One such type of knowledge is certainty. It is really certainty that the secular epistemologist struggles with the most. The Encyclopaedia Britannica discusses the views of G.E. Moore on knowledge and certainty thus:

In his 1941 paper ""Certainty,"" Moore observed that the word "certain" is commonly used in four main types of idiom: "I feel certain that," "I am certain that," "I know for certain that," and "It is certain that." He pointed out that there is at least one use of "I know for certain that p" and "It is certain that p" on which neither of these sentences can be true unless p is true. A sentence such as "I knew for certain that he would come but he didn't," for example, is self-contradictory, whereas "I felt certain he would come but he didn't" is not. On the basis of considerations like these, Moore contended that "a thing can't be certain unless it is known." It is this fact that distinguishes the concept of certainty from that of truth: "a thing that nobody knows may quite well be true, but cannot possibly be certain." Moore concluded that a necessary condition for the truth of "It is certain that p" is that somebody should know that p. Moore is therefore among the philosophers who answer in the negative the question of whether it is possible for p to be certain without being known.[5]

It would be fair to point out that not every philosopher would state with Moore that "It is not possible for *p* to be certain without being known". However, the discussion suggests a link between certainty and knowledge, and this link is of great interest to Christian apologists like myself.

The article goes on to discuss other aspects of the beginning of knowledge - though they do not use that term. They discuss the part played by empiricism and by rationalism. Knowledge due to empiricism implies that the knowledge can be achieved from first principles. It is observed, or measured. Discussions with atheists have suggested that many believe this knowledge to be based on the functioning of their senses. However, as a source of knowledge empiricism must be weak. Empiricism requires a starting point, or presupposition, and the presupposition on which the observations of senses is founded seems weak. How can one trust one's senses, when it can be easily demonstrated that senses can be manipulated, confused or deceived.

Rationalism also fails as a starting point for knowledge, however. Rationalism is certainly important, but, again, we need a starting point, on which reason is to be built. A famous example of this is the Euclidean axiom on which geometry is built, an implication of which is that the three angles of a triangle add up to 180° - the same as a straight line. Euclidean geometry seems to correspond to actual life, yet it is mathematically possible to develop non-Euclidean geometries, where the angles of a triangle do not add up to 180°. If we wish to know which geometry is "correct", neither an appeal to empiricism nor to reason will suffice.

Can You Be Sure of Anything You Know?

At the heart of the dilemma of the unbeliever is the problem of uncertainty. It is often thought that an atheist is someone who has definitely decided that there is no god - as far as they are concerned, the case is closed. An agnostic, on the other hand, believes that absolute certainty is not possible. Yet, it is becoming apparent that the absolute certainty of the atheist does not really bear examination. Even the world's best known atheist, Richard Dawkins, does not think that complete atheistic certainty is tenable.

Let us, then, take the idea of a spectrum of probabilities seriously, and place human judgements about the existence of God along it, between two extremes of opposite certainty. The spectrum is continuous, but it can be represented by the following seven milestones along the way.

1. *Strong theist. 100 per cent probability of God. In the words of C. G. Jung, 'I do not believe, I know!'*

2. *Very high probability but short of 100 per cent. De facto theist. 'I cannot know for certain, but I strongly believe in God and live my life on the assumption that he is there.'*

3. *Higher than 50 per cent but not very high. Technically agnostic but leaning towards theism. 'I am very uncertain, but I am inclined to believe in God.'*

4. *Exactly 50 per cent. Completely impartial agnostic. 'God's existence and non-existence are exactly equiprobable.'*

5. *Lower than 50 per cent but not very low. Technically agnostic but leaning towards atheism. 'I don't know whether God exists but I'm inclined to be sceptical.'*

6. *Very low probability, but short of zero. De facto atheist. 'I cannot know for certain but I think God is very improbable, and I live my life on the assumption that he is not there.'*

7. *Strong atheist. 'I know there is no God, with the same conviction as Jung "knows" there is one.'*

*I'd be surprised to meet many people in category 7, but I include it for symmetry with category 1, which is well populated. It is in the nature of faith that one is capable, like Jung, of holding a belief without adequate reason to do so (Jung also believed that particular books on his shelf spontaneously exploded with a loud bang). Atheists do not have faith; and reason alone could not propel one to total conviction that anything definitely does not exist. Hence category 7 is in practice rather emptier than its opposite number, category 1, which has many devoted inhabitants. I count myself in category 6, but leaning towards 7—I am agnostic only to the extent that I am agnostic about fairies at the bottom of the garden.*⁶

To be fair, Dawkins has allowed himself only a little uncertainty. When interviewed by Bill Maher, he has suggested that on this 7-point spectrum, he measures 6.9. But that small uncertainty is nevertheless uncertainty. What then occurs in conversation is that the atheist concludes, by analogy, that no one should be in category 1. As an aside, I should note that when people have told me that I cannot possibly know God for certain, I have pointed out that they are making a claim of certain knowledge over what is going on in my brain - a claim that is certainly not possible!

That being said, it is a point of principle that they cannot be sure about anything. We laugh at the following exchange, yet it has happened in actual fact to so many of us, that it underscores a common fallacy.

Opponent: We cannot be certain about anything we know.

Me: Are you sure about that?

Opponent: Yes!

This is usually followed up by the opponent saying, as reported above "But you can't know for certain either." At which point, we can point out that they are making a knowledge claim about what we know. This matter builds on our earlier platform, because, according to our paradigm, knowledge is from God, and therefore has a certain existence.

Even if I turn out to be wrong about a fact, my paradigm allows for absolute certainty, because of the absolute nature of God.

The question remains - "How can you be certain about anything that you know?"

The atheist maintains that it is not possible for anyone to be certain about anything that they know.

Two children are doing math homework. The question is "what is 5 times 8?".

Fred answers "45". Jim answers "60".

Who is the more correct?

Some of you might state that Fred is more correct, because his answer is closer to the correct answer. But your reasoning presupposes that the correct answer is an absolute value, which you know for certain. Of course, we are absolutely certain that both are wrong, and the math teacher will award no points to either. With the question framed as it is, Fred does not score a half point for being closer. As Dawkins himself claimed in a Tweet "'It may not be your truth but it's true for me. It's my truth.' No, if it's true it's true -- for everyone. Truth doesn't care about you."[7]

How much knowledge do you need to have to be certain? No one can claim to know even a small fraction of all the knowledge that there might be in the universe. So, the atheist would maintain that there always might be some knowledge that might contradict something that you thought you knew. So, the only way to know something for certain is if you know every single piece of knowledge that there is to know.

No - that is not the only way to be certain, actually. Suppose you know someone else, who knows everything there is to know, and you know that this other person never tells a lie. Then what He has told you, you can know for certain. And that is the position of the Christian. We know God, and He knows everything, so what God has chosen to reveal to us is absolutely certain. And that is where our presuppositions come from. God exists, and His Word is true.

---

[1] Rankin, R. (2012), *Study: Bible Engagement in Churchgoers' Hearts, Not Always Practiced*,
< http://www.lifeway.com/Article/research-survey-bible-engagement-churchgoers >, retrieved 1/6/2016

[2] Deuteronomy 6:6-9

[3] Judges 2:7-10

[4] Bahnsen, G.L. (1998), *Van Til's Apologetic: Readings and Analysis*, (Presbyterian & Reformed Publishing Company), pp4-7

5

[5] epistemology. 2016. *Encyclopædia Britannica Online,* < http://www.britannica.com/topic/epistemology > Retrieved 07 January, 2016

[6] Dawkins, Richard (2008-01-16). *The God Delusion* (pp. 73-74). Houghton Mifflin Harcourt. Kindle Edition. < https://twitter.com/richarddawkins/status/633871148179156992 >, retrieved 1/7/2016

06 Don't Apologize. Apologize.

> *And who is he who will harm you if you become followers*
> *of what is good? But even if you should suffer for*
> *righteousness' sake, you are blessed. "And do not be afraid of*
> *their threats, nor be troubled." But sanctify the Lord God in*
> *your hearts, and always be ready to give a defense to*
> *everyone who asks you a reason for the hope that is in you,*
> *with meekness and fear; having a good conscience, that when*
> *they defame you as evildoers, those who revile your good*
> *conduct in Christ may be ashamed. For it is better, if it is the*
> *will of God, to suffer for doing good than for doing evil.*[1]

Well, it's about time, I hear you say. You have been writing a book about apologetics, and you have reached chapter 6, and you have not yet commented on 1 Peter 3:15 - the very verse from which apologetics gets its name!

> *Always be ready to give a defense to everyone who asks*
> *you a reason for the hope that is in you.*

Some versions translate the word *defense* as *answer*. Both are possible. The Greek word is *apologia* (απολογια). The word looks like apology. In fact, the old meaning of the word apology is to make a defense, or an answer, or response. We are not saying sorry that we are Christians. We are not sorry about holding this faith, which we are telling people is the truth. Don't apologize. Instead, apologize. Defend. Answer.

Therefore, the practise of robustly defending the faith is known as *apologetics*.

Of course, it is normal to quote the phrase that begins "always be ready". Greg Bahnsen wrote a book on apologetics, entitled "Always Ready". The concept of apologetics seems to have stored up two opposite types of emotions.

There are some Christians who don't like apologetics. It sounds too much like judging people, and we're not supposed to judge, right?[2] Apologetics seems divisive. Apart from that, we are used to apologists being very clever people. They are the sort of super-Christians who debate atheists on TV. Apologetics requires knowing a lot about science, and art, and philosophy. It isn't a practise for you and I, is it?

Then there is another group of Christians who are fascinated by apologetics. They love to listen to or watch a testosterone-filled debate, where an atheist gets a good pasting. As you might guess, this group tend to be (though not exclusively) young and male.

It is because of these extremes that I have left the discussion of this verse until I could lay down sufficient foundation. And, even now, it would seem to be important to quote the verse within its context, because it is too often ripped out of context.

Is It All Greek?

Classical apologists have a particular line on the way this key verse should be interpreted. Most classical apologists will use an argument for God, based on the Kalam Cosmological Argument (KCA). This principle will be examined in more detail in the next chapter. For now, I want to look at the background to the use of KCA in apologetics, how apologists use such an argument, with reference to 1 Peter 3:15, and then give my reasons as to why I think this is not a valid use of 1 Peter 3:15.

William Lane Craig is probably the best known proponent of the Kalam Cosmological Argument. In *Reasonable Faith*, he maintains that similar arguments date back to Classical Greek times.

> *The cosmological argument assumes that something exists and argues from the existence of that thing to the existence of a First Cause or a Sufficient Reason of the cosmos. This argument has its roots in Plato and Aristotle and was developed by medieval Islamic, Jewish, and Christian thinkers. It has been defended by such great minds as Plato, Aristotle, ibn Sina, al-Ghazali, ibn Rushd, Maimonides, Anselm, Aquinas, Scotus, Descartes, Spinoza, Berkeley, Locke, and Leibniz.*[3]

As I said, I will address the substance of the argument later. For now, however, I want to note that Craig and others interpret the *defense* of the faith to be made in 1 Peter 3:15 as a Greek concept. They argue that the Greek word *apologia* is a familiar Greek concept. An example of how apology was used in Classical Greek is Plato's Apology, in which he envisages Socrates defending himself at his trial.[4] It is argued that similar styles of robust argument, using reasoning, can be made to defend the Christian faith and argue for the existence of God. It is to this tradition that classical apologists appeal.

The difficulty in working Christian apologetics into the classical tradition would seem to be the nature of the background to the New Testament. All but one of the writers of the New Testament were Jewish, not Greek. Granted, Paul had a considerable knowledge of Greek philosophy, and it is argued that his address at Mars Hill in Acts 17 would constitute a classical argument. I believe I can show that Paul's Mars Hill address is not, in fact, Greek in style, but in the key apologetics verse of 1 Peter 3:15, we are dealing with the theology of a Jewish fisherman. Indeed, there are numerous places in the New Testament where we meet Jewish thought, expressed in the Koine (common) Greek language used throughout the 27 books. So, it is my contention that the background to 1 Peter 3:15 is not Greek, but Jewish.

Peter and Isaiah
The above explains why 1 Peter 3:15 must be read in its proper context. I started this chapter by quoting from 1 Peter

3:13-17. Verse 13 emphasizes the blessing which we have as God's people. It would seem odd for Peter to segue from that to Greek philosophy. Indeed, one of the points that most apologists seem to miss is what comes immediately before the famous quotation.

"And do not be afraid of their threats, nor be troubled."[5]

The NKJV shows this as a quotation - and so it is. It is a quotation from Isaiah 8. Let's examine verses 12-13 more closely.

"Do not call conspiracy all that this people calls conspiracy, and do not fear what they fear, nor be in dread. But the LORD of hosts, him you shall honor as holy. Let him be your fear, and let him be your dread.[6]

As with 1 Peter 3:13ff, the context of Isaiah 8 is the assurance that we have, and not to be afraid of those who oppose us. This sounds like a form of apologetics! Indeed, in verse 13, we are told to honor the Lord as holy. This is the same instruction as we receive in the neglected first clause of 1 Peter 3:15 - "honor Christ as holy" (ESV). The word "Christ" does not appear in the *textus receptus*, and hence not in the KJV or NKJV. However, the ESV, NASB and others include it (it is in early Greek manuscripts), and the parallel with Isaiah 8 is striking. The coincidence is too great to be missed. This close relationship between 1 Peter 3:15 and Isaiah 8:12-13 suggests two corollaries.

1. Peter is emphasizing that Christ is indeed LORD.

2. The *apologia* of 1 Peter 3:15 does not hark back to Greek philosophy. Instead it harks back to the prophecies of Isaiah.

Yet, Classical Apologetics is built entirely on a structure of the application of Greek philosophy to the defense of the Christian faith. For this reason, arguments are built for the existence of God, based on empiricism. It is my contention, in this book, that this approach is fundamentally flawed, and I will critique some of the traditional arguments used by Classical Apologists in the next chapter. In fact, Apologetics should be founded on an expository tradition, founded on both Testaments of the Bible. In the model that I am supporting, the use of the Bible in apologetics is not only to be encouraged, I argue that apologetics is incorrect, if it fails to use the Bible. That is why the approach that I favor would often be referred to as Presuppositional Apologetics, because of its twin presuppositions that God exists and that the Bible is true. Indeed, it is presuppositional - though I do not accept all the extraneous baggage sometimes associated with Presuppositional Apologetics. I note that other writers have used other terms such as Biblical Apologetics[7] or Expository

Apologetics[8]. These are both terms that I prefer, but the expression Presuppositional Apologetics has become well known, and it, too, truthfully describes my approach, so I will continue to use it.

---

[1] 1 Peter 3:13-17

[2] Yes, we are - but that would be a bunny trail at this point, so I won't answer myself just yet!

[3] Craig, William Lane (2008). Reasonable Faith (3rd edition): Christian Truth and Apologetics (p. 96). Crossway. Kindle Edition.

[4] Plato. 2016. Encyclopædia Britannica Online. Retrieved 08 January, 2016, from < http://www.britannica.com/biography/Plato >

[5] 1 Peter 3:14

[6] Isaiah 8:12-13 (ESV)

[7] Clifford B MacManis

[8] Voddie Baucham Jr

07 Defending a Probable God

A Psalm of Thanksgiving. Make a joyful shout to the LORD, all you lands! Serve the LORD with gladness; Come before His presence with singing. Know that the LORD, He is God; It is He who has made us, and not we ourselves; We are His people and the sheep of His pasture. Enter into His gates with thanksgiving, And into His courts with praise. Be thankful to Him, and bless His name. For the LORD is good; His mercy is everlasting, And His truth endures to all generations.[1]

The Bible is not a book of debate. It is not a high school essay.

When you write high school essays, you need to marshal the arguments in favor of your proposition and against it. Having weighed all these things carefully, your conclusion gives you the opportunity to advance your opinion, backed up by the careful analysis preceding.

The Bible does not discuss the existence of God. It starts with the phrase "In the beginning, God..." In fact, the only mention of the possible non-existence of God is found in Psalm 14:1, and repeated in Psalm 53:1:

The fool says in his heart "There is no God".

In Psalm 100, we are supplied with a command:- "Know that the LORD, He is God." The Psalm continues "It is He who has made us, and not we ourselves". This Psalm, like the rest of the Bible, assumes that the existence of God is self-evident, and that it does not require proof.

However, the job of the Classical Apologist seems to be to prove that God exists. It appears that their route towards defending Christianity is two-fold.

1. Prove beyond all doubt that a god exists.

2. Prove that the god which exists has to be the God of the Bible.

It is notable, however, that some apologists concentrate only on step 1. It is often considered enough to prove that a god exists, and that people can then make the leap to decide that this god must be God. There are several methods of attempting to make this proof. For example, there is the argument from design - that every building must have a builder and every painting must have a painter. The technical term for this is the Teleological Argument. This argument was expressed most famously by the 18th Century Anglican clergyman William Paley in his famous book *Natural Theology*, which we will discuss later. One much used early extra-biblical argument for the existence of God is the Ontological Argument.

The Ontological Argument

The Ontological Argument was probably explained earliest by an Archbishop of Canterbury, who lived a thousand years ago, by the name of Anselm (1033-1109). In his book, Proslogion, Anselm conducts a thought experiment. He tries to imagine God, and what He might be like. He then assumes that, because he can imagine God, then God must exist, and that He must be at least as great as Anselm can imagine, but probably greater.

> *Hence, even the fool is convinced that something exists in the understanding, at least, than which nothing greater can be conceived. For, when he hears of this, he understands it. And whatever is understood, exists in the understanding. And assuredly that, than which nothing greater can be conceived, cannot exist in the understanding alone. For, suppose it exists in the understanding alone: then it can be conceived to exist in reality; which is greater.*

> *Therefore, if that, than which nothing greater can be conceived, exists in the understanding alone, the very being, than which nothing greater can be conceived, is one, than which a greater can be conceived. But obviously this is impossible. Hence, there is doubt that there exists a being, than which nothing greater can be conceived, and it exists both in the understanding and in reality.*[2]

The being that Anselm could envisage, however, could not possibly be God. If we could think it, then it couldn't be God. Moreover, the attributes of God are found in the Bible. What might be found in the mind is capable of being twisted by the world, the flesh or the devil.

> "For My thoughts are not your thoughts, Nor are your ways
> My ways," says the LORD. "For as the heavens are higher
> than the earth, So are My ways higher than your ways, And
> My thoughts than your thoughts."[3]

The *otherness* of God, and the impossibility of thinking towards Him, is emphasized in Psalm 50.

> These things you have done, and I kept silent; You thought
> that I was altogether like you; But I will rebuke you, And set
> them in order before your eyes.[4]

Another common argument is the Cosmological Argument, which looks for a cause for everything, and suggests that the cause must be a god. There is also a moral argument, that the existence of good can only be possible because of God. Indeed, there are many different arguments for God, one of which is even presented as a wager[5], but the most common one among modern Classical Apologists is the Kalam Cosmological Argument - a refinement of the simple cosmological argument. This argument for God, often referred to by its initials (KCA), is used by a number of apologists, who may or may not state the name of the argument, but has probably been explained in the most detail by its most fervent supporter, William Lane Craig.

The Kalam Cosmological Argument

Craig, in his book *reasonable Faith*, states the "proof" in the following syllogism:

The kalam cosmological argument may be formulated as follows:

1. *Whatever begins to exist has a cause.*

2. *The universe began to exist.*

3. *Therefore, the universe has a cause.*[6]

The starting point for Lane's argument is that he believes the first premise is self-evident.

Premise (1) seems obviously true—at the least, more so than its negation. First and foremost, it's rooted in the metaphysical intuition that something cannot come into being from nothing. To suggest that things could just pop into being uncaused out of nothing is to quit doing serious metaphysics and to resort to magic. Second, if things really could come into being uncaused out of nothing, then it becomes inexplicable why just anything and everything do not come into existence uncaused from nothing. Finally, the

first premise is constantly confirmed in our experience.
Atheists who are scientific naturalists thus have the strongest
of motivations to accept it.[7]

Lane then spends many pages, locking horns with a variety of atheists who deny premise 1, which he believes is self-evident. After all this argument, which becomes highly sophisticated, including a discussion on the mathematical difference between an actual infinity and a potential infinity, all he has achieved is to prove, in his own mind, that the universe has a cause, and he presumes that cause to be a "god".

It sounds as if I am about to dismiss a huge chunk of Lane's discussion as if it were wrong. I am not dismissing it on those grounds. I am dismissing it from this portion of my book, on the grounds that the evidence that he provides is irrelevant. The fact that he has to address the objections of so many atheists to arguments that he makes indicates that he is on the wrong path. It is not that his discussion is uninteresting. There is a different context, to be discussed later in this book, where his discussion will be relevant. But it is not relevant as a proof of God, because it self-evidently fails.

Following Lane's long defense of the first premise, he then spends a considerable amount of time, analyzing the conclusion (3), that "the universe has a cause", and tries to discuss the nature of that cause (i.e. God) without reference to the Bible.

> *On the basis of a conceptual analysis of the conclusion implied by the kalam cosmological argument, we may therefore infer that a personal Creator of the universe exists, who is uncaused, beginningless, changeless, immaterial, timeless, spaceless, and unimaginably powerful. This, as Thomas Aquinas was wont to remark, is what everybody means by "God."*[8]

With respect, this is not what is meant by "God". Indeed, the idea of what is meant by "God", in quotation marks, is irrelevant. I am not interested in "God". I am interested in God. Non of this extra-biblical discussion reveals God to be loving, holy, merciful, or, for that matter, angry with sin. Yet, we must remind ourselves, that these things are precisely what the apostle Paul has told us are part of the nature of God, revealed to every single person who lives, from the creation of the world. In other words, the Kalam Cosmological god does not have the complete nature of the God of the Bible. Therefore, the KCA god is not the same as the God of the Bible. Therefore, the KCA god is a false god and an idol.

Now, I am aware that this makes some people angry. Am I saying that Lane does not believe in the God of the Bible? No, I am not saying that. And there are many Classical Apologists, who will do precisely the right thing in showing Christians from the Bible what God is like. I am simply pointing out that their argument for the existence of God is fallacious, wrong and unbiblical. It does not prove God. If it proves anything - and I have my doubts - it proves a form of theism; the existence of a probable god. The God of the Bible is not a probable god. He is the only God.

The Teleological Argument

In a further chapter, Lane discusses the teleological argument. This is also known as the argument from design. Now, I get a bit red in the face, thinking about this argument, because I have used this argument myself many times in the past. Let me explain how I used to use the teleological argument in one of my first creation talks. The entirety of the argument from the next sub-heading, to the one after it, is an argument that I would no longer use. So I am going to tell you what I used to say, then self-critique it.

Materials by Design

When I was a Head of Science in a comprehensive school in Wales (this is the sort of school that would be called a Public High School in the US), I was responsible for purchasing furniture and equipment for a new science laboratory. This laboratory was going to be used primarily for Chemistry. It was replacing an old laboratory, which had wooden tables. Over the years, these tables had soaked all sorts of noxious chemicals into them, as well as ink from the pens of children, intent on graffiti. The removal of the latter could only really be done effectively with sandpaper, which obviously removed much of the wooden surface as well. The wooden surface had also been damaged by spillages of organic solvents, and nitric acid. Other damage had been caused by burns, from bunsen burners and their lighters.

The new tables that I chose were covered with a brand new material. I cannot now recall the name of this material, but it had been specially developed for use in school science laboratories. A team of scientists had obviously thought carefully through the properties that this material needed. These thoughts must have influenced their design brief.

The material needs to be unreactive. It should not burn, if touched by lit wooden burners or natural gas bunsen burners. It would need to be resistant to spillages by nitric acid (which can oxidize wood) and organic solvents. It would also be non-absorbent to ink. If permanent marker ink were used, then it should be possible for the surface to resist a cleaning solvent, such as ethanol. In extreme cases, it would be good if the surface could be rubbed with sandpaper, without causing the surface to be rough. The surface material should not, however, be so slippy that students' notebooks could not easily be rested on it. Finally, and just as important, it should be attractive to look at - preferably with a mock-stone effect, such as granite.

Imagine another design brief for a liquid material to cover a large amount of our planet.

It should be a good solvent for ionic electrolytes. It's molecules should be small enough to cross semi-permeable membranes (e.g. cell walls), yet should be able to associate with each other to provide a higher effective molecular mass, causing the melting point and boiling point to be much higher than similar tiny molecules (hydrogen-bonding). Most liquids contract as they cool, so that when they freeze, the solid material forms at the bottom of the liquid. However, this special liquid should be designed so that as it decreases in temperature, its last few degrees before freezing should cause it actually to expand, so that the solid form actually floats on the liquid. This is important, so that it can form floating icebergs, and ponds can freeze on the top, sheltering the fish underneath. As you have realized, we are talking about water, and there is so much of it on this planet that we forget that its anomalous expansion before freezing is unique, and, if it were not, life would not survive. The actual temperature range of the liquid phase - the difference between boiling point and freezing point - should be sufficiently narrow for all three phases to co-exist easily on the same planet.

My talk would be rounded up by pointing out that water - like the laboratory surfaces - is clearly a designed material. Its designer must be God. Therefore God exists!

Critique of Materials by Design

There are some aspects of this account which are completely acceptable, in the right context. The problem with the argument is that it does not prove God. Why should it? All I have done is suggest that water looks like a substance, which has been intelligently designed. But if that is all I have done, I have done nothing. As I said, the problem is one of context.

To illustrate what I mean, let's alter the above argument. Let's start with the description of the laboratory surface material. Now let me remind you of our previous studies about the nature of God. He is a good God, and the Creator. These two qualities (which are, of course, by no means His only qualities) suggest that He would design a material like water precisely how He did. Then we might end the session, which has concentrated on the fact of God being Creator, by praising Him for how He has worked in even these seemingly insignificant details.

Now that would rescue my talk. Except, my talk would no longer be a proof of God! But then it never was a good proof of God. It suggested the existence of a "god", but said nothing about His nature. With this latter change, we start with the presupposition of God, and the truth of His word, and we see that being applied to this otherwise rather mundane part of chemical engineering. So this is not a proof of God. It is the corollary of what we expect, given what we have learned of God from Scripture.

And now we see precisely my problem with this teleological argument, and also for the kalam cosmological argument. In both cases, the discussions of the technical sciences would be very interesting, if we did not try to use them as proofs of God, but rather as examples of the outworking of the correct presuppositions.

This is precisely the same issue with the old method of stating that:

"Every painting has a painter, and every building has a builder"

We suggest scenarios where someone throws paint randomly over a canvas. We do not expect that to form the Mona Lisa. Or we have an explosion in a brick factory. We do not expect that to produce a great building. Therefore, we say, the creation must have had a creator.

The problem with the argument is that it does not point us to the true god of the Bible. It simply points us to a "god", and is therefore just an idol. My friend Sye ten Bruggencate is fond of reminding his audiences, when he lectures on this subject, that "God is not A builder. He is THE builder."

So, the argument is the wrong way round. It is not wrong to look at creation, and marvel that it is so well made. But we know it is well made, because we know the Creator, not the other way around.

In fact, most of the Classical Apologists who use these arguments are really Presuppositional Apologists in their heads! Lee Strobel uses the film "The Case for a Creator" (and the book of the same title) to chart his journey from childish faith, to atheism, and to genuine faith as a Christian. He claims that he was following the evidence where it led. But he only followed the evidence to God, because deep within, he actually knew that God existed, and he began to apply what he had learned previously, to the "new" evidence that he found. I would not doubt his salvation at all. I simply don't think that evidence really led him to Christ, as he claims. His brain interpreted the evidence correctly, given a presupposition of God, that he had not realized that he had! As Sye also says about such conversions, which he also treats as genuine - "God is able to strike a straight blow with a bent stick".

The Moral Argument

There are those who have advanced what might be termed a *moral* argument for the existence of God. Lane is helpful in understanding the substance of this argument.

The moral argument for the existence of God implies the existence of a Being that is the embodiment of the ultimate Good, which is the source of the objective moral values we experience in the world. The reasoning at the heart of the moral argument goes all the way back to Plato, who argued that things have goodness insofar as they stand in some relation to the Good, which subsists in itself. With the advent of Christian theism, the Good became identified with God himself.[9]

Thus, the existence of so much good in the world can only be explained by stating that there is a god who made it all, and that god must be good.

It surprises me that Christians would advance this argument. It is rather like the boxer who leads with his chin. In response, it would seem completely fair, in this context, for the unbeliever to bring up the old chestnut: "If God is a God of love, why is there so much suffering in the world?"

Of course, most people who advance the negative argument do not want to hear a reasoned answer. It is usually an attempt to shut the Christian up. In most circumstances, the question is unfair, but it strikes me as actually very fair, in the context of someone trying to prove that God exists because good exists. It does not tackle the problem of the existence or origin of evil - a concept known in philosophy as *theodicy.*

In his book, *Moral values and the Idea of God*, William Sorley summarizes "proofs" of God prevalent in his day, such as the Ontological Argument, the Cosmological Argument and the Teleological Argument, and dismissed each one. He then proceeds to argue for the obvious existence of good and evil. His argument is that evil is evil to us because of context. He seems to take a view that, what is evil in one context might actually be acceptable in another.

> *If the reasoner starts from the power, goodness, and intelligence of man and argues that God must therefore be powerful, good, and intelligent, only in a higher indeed an infinite degree, then the procedure is anthropomorphic, and we may say that man is making God after his own image. There may be apologies for this procedure, for at least it is true that there is no higher object immediately known to man than the human mind, and it is therefore more reasonable to hold that God is like man than that he resembles other created things. But it is not the procedure that has been adopted in this book. We have not argued that God is good because we find goodness in man, but that he is good because we find the idea of goodness to be valid for that universal order which we are trying to understand. And we speak of his wisdom and his power, not because man has some share of these qualities, but because they are implied in that*

*conception of the world as purposive which is necessary to
explain the relation of the order of nature to the moral order.[10]*

Sorley is arguing that there is a reality to the existence of a
moral order, just as there is a reality to the existence of
scientific laws. Therefore, this moral order can only be
explained by a personal, moral god, who is good.

The problem with the argument is much the same as the
problems we have had with the other arguments. The
argument from morality really works at its best, when we start
from a presupposition of the existence of God and the truth of
His word! Morality does not explain or prove God. When I was
studying for my Masters in Education, the first seminar series
that I attended was led by a professor (at the University of
Manchester) who was an atheist, and, apparently, an expert in
ethics - the subject which atheists like to use to substitute for
morality. He argued that morality, or rather positive ethics,
emanated from an evolutionary view of society, and how
people reacted to each other. He would, quite rightly, be able
to advance his society ethics as a reasonable explanation, at
the same level as Sorley's moral god. That God is good is not
seen because there is a world of good and evil. It is the other
way around. Good and evil are defined in terms of their
acceptance of, or opposition to, the character and nature of
God.

Natural Theology

A convenient heading, under which all of these naturalistic and evidential arguments for God may be placed, is the heading *Natural Theology*. The undoubted hero of Natural Theology, which includes the types of proofs for God, at which we have looked in this chapter, was William Paley (1743 - 1805). His magnum opus was the book of the same title. He was a professor at the University of Cambridge, as well as an Anglican clergyman (in fact Cambridge University teachers had to be Anglican clergymen in those days), and therefore his ideas were influential on a later young Cambridge undergraduate, interested in natural history, but studying theology - one Charles Darwin. Darwin was impressed by these naturalistic arguments for God, but, as he later came to see the flaws in the argument, the God that he later rejected was the God of *Natural Theology*, rather than the God of the Bible. There is a distinction, as we shall see.

Paley is famous for his watchmaker analogy, which is really an argument from design. We shall allow him to relate the argument in his own words.

> In crossing a heath, suppose I pitched my foot against a stone, and were asked how the stone came to be there, I might possibly answer, that for any thing I knew to the contrary it had lain there for ever ; nor would it, perhaps, be very easy to show the absurdity of this answer. But suppose I had found a watch upon the ground, and it should be inquired how the

watch happened to be in that place, I should hardly think of the answer which I had before given, that for anything I knew the watch might have always been there. Yet why should not this answer serve for the watch as well as for the stone; why is it not as admissible in the second case as in the first ? For this reason, and for no other, namely, that when we come to inspect the watch, we perceive — what we could not discover in the stone — that its several parts are framed and put together for a purpose, e.g. that they are so formed and adjusted as to produce motion, and that motion so regulated as to point out the hour of the day; that if the different parts had been differently shaped from what they are, or placed after any other manner or in any other order than that in which they are placed, either no motion at all would have been carried on in the machine, or none which would have answered the use that is now served by it.[11]

This is a very clear argument from design. Yet, it is well known that atheists, such as Richard Dawkins, reject it. Dawkins argues that the appearance of design does not imply actual design. For this reason, Dawkins entitled one of his books *The Blind Watchmaker*. While we might find Paley's arguments more convincing than Dawkins, this is because we start with the correct presupposition. The watch, in fact, only looks designed, given the presupposition that there is a designer. Once again, this is not a proof of God. Paley's book is detailed. He even uses natural history to describe what he thinks about the nature, goodness and personality of God. Yet in each of these arguments, they only stand up, given the paradigm in which Paley was writing - one of a vaguely Christian consensus.

When I published an edition of Paley's *Natural Theology*, I included a Preface, in which I explained some of my objections to the methodology. Given that there are no copyright implications, it might be useful to record at length some of the comments I made then.

William Paley's book, Natural Theology, is a work of monumental importance. It has been hugely influential in the field of natural sciences - especially Biology - even though the majority of people have never heard of it. Published in 1802, it purports to give "evidences of the existence and attributes of the Deity".

In Paley's time, Natural Theology was an established field of study, though it is now either neglected or known under another name. It can be defined as "the branch of philosophy and theology which attempts to prove God's existence, define God's attributes, or derive correct doctrine based solely from human reason and/or observations of the natural world." If classical theology is concerned with a study of the scriptures, then natural theology is the attempt to derive theological ideas from nature, without reference to scripture.

One of the main reasons for the importance of Paley's book is its position in the history of science. Paley was teaching at Cambridge University when Charles Darwin was a student. Darwin was much taken with the concept of natural theology, and, though he was otherwise considered to be a poor student, Paley's natural theology course was one in which Darwin excelled. The particular type of "proofs" offered by Paley's work may have had an influence on Darwin's eventual rejection of divine origin as an explanation for life.[12]

There is a sense in which Paley's arguments on their own lack authority. That is not to say that they are not persuasive. Rather, they make more sense with a starting point or presupposition that the Bible is true. Proverbs has a warning for those who would suppose that their own arguments, without scripture, can be sufficient - "Trust in the LORD with all your heart, And lean not on your own understanding". (Proverbs 3:5) This is an inadequacy of the field of natural theology. Although Romans 1 shows us that creation exists to point us to the creator, the theology that we thus derive condemns rather than saves.

For since the creation of the world His invisible attributes are clearly seen, being understood by the things that are made, even His eternal power and Godhead, so that they are without excuse, because, although they knew God, they did not glorify Him as God, nor were thankful, but became futile in their thoughts, and their foolish hearts were darkened. (Romans 1:20-21)

In conclusion, we see that an argument from design is insufficient, because it only leads so far, and can never lead to the person who God really is. For the latter, we need words of revelation in the Bible, which should be our foundation. Nevertheless, it is instructive that, starting from nature, an early 19th century writer can be so sure that God is behind everything in the universe, when one of his students should later be so adamant that nothing was due to divine fiat. For this reason alone, Paley's Natural Theology deserves to be better known. Its arguments may be insufficient – yet they are head and shoulders above those of Darwin. Darwin's theories have persisted only because they attempt to explain origins in a way which does not require God – and a rebellious world prefers to consider itself unbeholden to God, so that they do not have to submit to His authority. In that wish, they will ultimately be disappointed, as:

At the name of Jesus every knee should bow, of those in heaven, and of those on earth, and of those under the earth, and that every tongue should confess that Jesus Christ is Lord, to the glory of God the Father. (Philippians 2:10-11)[13]

Does It Matter?

You might be wondering, then, if it really matters what method we use, if God can use the evidential method. I suggest that it matters a great deal. It is our responsibility to do things the way God requires, not by our own methods. The reason why the KCA or the teleological argument, or other arguments sometimes work is because there are other factors, which have developed a de facto, while unrecognized, presupposition of God. It is far better therefore, indeed much more biblical therefore, to argue presuppositionally, rather than evidentially. The presuppositional method gives the glory to God - precisely what Romans 1 tells us that the unbeliever is refusing to do. The evidential method does not give glory to God, so is working by precisely the method that the unbeliever prefers.

The reason why it matters that we don't use the evidential method inherent in Classical Apologetics is because of at whom it is aimed. The evidence, which is so beautiful to those of us who love the Lord already, is aimed at unbelievers. It has rightly been pointed out that evidence is something that is offered in a courtroom to a judge and jury, in order for them to make a decision. When we use Classical Apologetics, who are we directing the evidence at? The unbeliever. Therefore, who are we implying is the judge? We are making the unbeliever both the judge and jury. And who is on trial? God is on trial. There is something wrong with this scenario.

Classical Apologetics uses the unbeliever as a judge. The Bible says that the unbeliever is a fool. Classical Apologetics has appointed a fool as the judge, and we wonder why we get foolish verdicts!

Classical Apologetics puts God in the dock. The Bible says "You shall not put the Lord your God to the test".[14]

Sye ten Bruggencate puts it thus:

> Imagine someone came up to you and said "I don't believe in words". We'd think that they were a fool. We wouldn't believe them and we wouldn't take out our dictionary to give them evidence. But if someone came up to you and said "I don't believe in God", we believe them, we give them evidence and we don't think they're a fool, when the Bible calls them fools! Something has gone wrong.[15]

Something has indeed gone wrong - and that is the motivation for my writing this book.

I have been somewhat negative in this chapter, criticizing Classical Apologetics and its methodology. I should not continue that criticism, without offering a positive opinion on what we actually **should** do instead, and that is what the next chapter is about.

---

[1] Psalm 100

[2] Anselm of Canterbury. *Anselm's Proslogium or Discourse on the Existence of God*, Medieval Sourcebook. Sidney N. Deane (trans.). Fordham University Center for Medieval Studies. < http://www.fordham.edu/halsall/basis/anselm-proslogium.html >, Retrieved 1/11/2016.

[3] Isaiah 55:8-9

[4] Psalm 50:21

[5] Pascal's Wager

[6] Craig, William Lane (2008). *Reasonable Faith (3rd edition): Christian Truth and Apologetics* (p. 111). Crossway. Kindle Edition.

[7] *ibid*

[8] *ibid, p154*

[9] *ibid, p104*

[10] Sorley, W. R. (William Ritchie), 1855-1935. Moral values and the idea of God : The Gifford lectures delivered in the University of Aberdeen in 1914 and 1915 (Kindle Locations 6893-6900). Cambridge [Eng.] : University Press.

[11] Paley, W (1803), ed. Taylor, P. (2009), *Natural Theology*, (J6D Publications),p1

[12] *Ibid, p i*

[13] *Ibid, p iv-v*

[14] Deuteronomy 6:16 (ESV), repeated by Jesus, to the devil, at Matthew 4:7

[15] From the movie *How to Answer the Fool*, featuring Sye ten

08 Don't Answer. Answer.

Classical Apologetics has suggested that the unbeliever can be persuaded towards, at the very least, a form of theism. We have spent the last chapter suggesting that this is not, in fact, the biblical approach.

In 2007, the atheist, Antony Flew, stopped being an atheist, and became a deist.[1] He published a book, entitled *There is a god*. Many Christians seemed to be jumping up and down with excitement at his pronouncement. Other Christians, however, were not so comfortable. I was in the latter category, as was Lita Cosner of Creation Ministries International, who wrote:

> *Some of the attributes of the god that Flew acknowledges are also attributes of God, but Flew does not acknowledge the Trinity or Christ as the second Person of the Trinity, both of which are essential Christian doctrines. So although Flew's deistic beliefs echo Christian belief in some areas, the god he accepts is not the same as the God of the Bible, although he professes to remain open to the evidence. Flew never claims to be Christian; he is a self-identified deist who does not believe in an afterlife.*[2]

Flew has now entered that after life. While I will acknowledge the usual pious hope that Flew might have had a death-bed conversion, it seems unlikely that he did so - in which case, his "faith" in a sort-of god would not have saved him from Hell. I am aware that the previous sentence may offend some, where the prevailing evangelical jargon is to hope that he gave his life to Jesus just before he died. The prevalence of that convenient formula, however Flew's "spiritual" journey, such as it was, was entirely due to the sort of arguments that Classical Apologists promote. Of course, plenty of others, who have heard the Classical Apologists arguments, have been saved, but this is in spite of the methodology, not because of it. It is God who ultimately chooses if the spiritual eyes of an unbeliever are going to be opened.

So, having waded through my arguments against the methodologies of the classical Apologist, you might now be thinking "All right, clever clogs. You've told us what not to do. Now tell us what we **should** do." So that is what I will attempt here.

Shall We Be Neutral?

During my years of teaching science in government schools in the UK[3], I frequently came across the argument of neutrality. The plea for neutrality comes from all sides. It frequently happens that unbelievers will request that we prove our case, without using the Bible. On the surface, this might sound fair to some. Indeed, I frequently get emails from people, asking me to provide information in this way: "My uncle wants me to prove that God exists, without using the Bible. What can I say to him?" Sometimes, I will explain the presuppositional method, and receive the reply "but my uncle is highly intelligent. I need to prove the Bible to him first." This latter sort of comment is very common, but shows that the questioner has not understood the issue. We have seen from Romans 1 that God exists, whether the unbeliever chooses to acknowledge this or not, and they do indeed actually know this fact. Therefore, to attempt to prove the existence of God without using the Bible is like trying to prove the existence of air without breathing.

We need to understand why this process is fundamentally flawed. Let us suppose that there were indeed a piece of evidence that would prove to the unbeliever, beyond doubt, that the Bible were true. Let's call this particular evidence the *silver bullet*. So many Christians want to know what this silver bullet is. Well, what if the silver bullet existed?

One day, when I was a High School science teacher, I was teaching a class about atoms. The school day was about to end at 3:30pm, and it was 3:25, as I was rounding up the lesson, when one girl challenged me. "I can't believe in these atoms," she said. "How do I know they are there?" There was no way that the rest of the class wanted to remain late to hear the answer, so I lent the girl a textbook to take home, to read the section about atoms. The same class was scheduled for my laboratory first thing the next morning. So, when they filed in, the girl gave me the textbook back. "Thanks, sir", she began. "That makes sense. I believe in atoms now!"

So, who had the greater authority - me, or the textbook author? Clearly, the textbook author had the greater authority. She could not believe in atoms on my say so, but after reading the textbook, she believed.

Now, consider the silver bullet evidence again. Remember, we are assuming that this silver bullet proves beyond doubt that the Bible is true. Once he has been furnished with this evidence, the young man's uncle above will say "Now I believe in God, because you have proved that the Bible is true." But, if this scenario were possible, what would have the greater authority, the Bible or the silver bullet? By definition, it would have to be the silver bullet, because the uncle could not believe in the Bible without the silver bullet.

But the Bible claims that it is the ultimate authority.[4] The Bible is the foundation, on which all other arguments are built. It is the lens, though which all other ideas are interpreted or judged. If we agree not to use the Bible as the basis for our perspectives, then we are not actually being neutral. We have, in fact, conceded the central point that the Bible is not necessary. Voddie Baucham comments:

We must be aware that many people will view the mere fact that we are using the Bible at all as questionable. In other words, we are assuming that the Bible is the authority in a debate about whether such an authority exists. Some suggest that the best course of action is to abandon the Bible, at least for a time, until we can establish common ground. I say this is disastrous. Doing so would be an admission of defeat. Our interlocutors are allowed to keep their presuppositions regardless of where the conversation goes. If we abandon ours, we have conceded the most crucial point. We must do no such thing![5]

I sat, open-mouthed in amazement, as I watched a YouTube video clip, showing one well-known apologist proclaiming "If we want to prove the Bible to be true, what can't we use? That's right! The Bible!" If we follow this methodology, then, at a stroke, we give up the very matter that we are supposed to be defending. The idea that there is neutral ground is not a neutral concept. It is a concept in opposition to biblical truth. According to our Lord, there is no neutral ground.

For he who is not against us is on our side.[6]

He who is not with Me is against Me, and he who does not gather with Me scatters.[7]

Of course, the Classical Apologist tells us that what they want is not neutral ground, but common ground. However, we already have common ground with the unbeliever. According to Romans 1, the unbeliever already knows that God exists, and in Romans 2 we read that he has a conscience, which informs him on moral issues.

> *For when Gentiles, who do not have the law, by nature do the things in the law, these, although not having the law, are a law to themselves, who show the work of the law written in their hearts, their conscience also bearing witness, and between themselves their thoughts accusing or else excusing them.*[8]

Neutral ground is not common ground, and should not be used as such, because, to repeat, neutral ground does not actually exist.

Don't Answer

The strategy that I am going to outline now has been well expressed by Presuppositional Apologists. Bahnsen has referred to it as a two-step process. This concept of a two-step process has been criticized elsewhere, because the strategy depends on two verses from the book of Proverbs. They are these:

> *4. Do not answer a fool according to his folly, Lest you also be like him.*

> *5. Answer a fool according to his folly, Lest he be wise in his own eyes.*[9]

One criticism of the approach suggests that the verses are taken out of context, and that they are not to be used to describe two separate strategies.[10] I am all in favor of making sure we do not quote verses out of context, so let's look at a little context.

Proverbs 26:1-12

1. As snow in summer and rain in harvest, So honor is not fitting for a fool.

2. Like a flitting sparrow, like a flying swallow, So a curse without cause shall not alight.

3. A whip for the horse, A bridle for the donkey, And a rod for the fool's back.

4. Do not answer a fool according to his folly, Lest you also be like him.

5. Answer a fool according to his folly, Lest he be wise in his own eyes.

6. He who sends a message by the hand of a fool Cuts off his own feet and drinks violence.

7. Like the legs of the lame that hang limp Is a proverb in the mouth of fools.

8. Like one who binds a stone in a sling Is he who gives honor to a fool.

9. Like a thorn that goes into the hand of a drunkard Is a proverb in the mouth of fools.

10. The great God who formed everything Gives the fool his hire and the transgressor his wages.

11. As a dog returns to his own vomit, So a fool repeats his folly.

12. Do you see a man wise in his own eyes? There is more hope for a fool than for him.

Two things stand out about this passage immediately. The first is that these proverbs are all separate sayings. The second is that all these proverbs refer to fools. It follows that we should not use verses 4-5 outside the concept referring to fools. However, they can be tackled separately, in the same way that verses 1 and 9 are related, but not linked.

With that contextual comment made, we will apply ourselves to Proverbs 26:4.

Do not answer a fool according to his folly, Lest you also be like him.

It is our contention that there is no neutral ground. Therefore, any argument that we give in an apologetic scenario, will either build on our presupposition or that of the unbeliever. If we build on the presupposition of the unbeliever, then we become like him. In other words, we adopt his foolishness. As we have discussed from Romans 1, the unbeliever is not really an unbeliever - he knows that God exists. Therefore, if we stand on his platform, we deny the God, whom we serve. That is why we become like him.

In what ways might we be guilty of so doing? Paul's closing exhortation in his first letter to Timothy is relevant in this context.

> *Command those who are rich in this present age not to be haughty, nor to trust in uncertain riches but in the living God, who gives us richly all things to enjoy. Let them do good, that they be rich in good works, ready to give, willing to share, storing up for themselves a good foundation for the time to come, that they may lay hold on eternal life. O Timothy! Guard what was committed to your trust, avoiding the profane and idle babblings and contradictions of what is falsely called knowledge—by professing it some have strayed concerning the faith. Grace be with you. Amen.*[11]

Paul begins this final section, maintaining that Timothy should be *commanding* unbelievers, rather than empathizing with them. Paul exhorts Timothy to avoid "profane and idle babblings". These are the foolish arguments, based on an unbiblical presupposition. That is why such knowledge that an unbeliever may appear to exhibit is actually "falsely called knowledge". The clue given about the nature of this knowledge is that such false knowledge involves "contradictions". We will see more of this in a moment.

In view of the verses from 1 Timothy, we can see that we should be inviting unbelievers to follow our arguments, from our presuppositions. At the very least, they ought to be able to see that our arguments are logically sound. Of course, their acceptance of such arguments will have nothing to do with either logic, or persuasiveness. We need at all times to remember that the unbeliever's acceptance of our arguments will only come by the Holy Spirit opening his eyes.

Answer

Without understanding the application of these verses in Proverbs, it might appear that verses 4 and 5 are contradictory.

Answer a fool according to his folly, Lest he be wise in his own eyes.

It is clear, however, that they cannot be contradictory. When Solomon was putting these verses into place, a man of his greatness would not have overlooked the apparent contrariness of the verses. More importantly, we must not forget that these verses were placed just so by the inspiration of the Holy Spirit. It is more logical, therefore, to suppose that this apparent contradiction is deliberate. Solomon is making a very deliberate point. We have just seen that we should not advance an argument from so-called neutral ground. What is being suggested in verse 5, therefore, is that we temporarily build an argument, based on an unbeliever's presupposition, for the sole purpose of showing him that the apparent wisdom of such a position is foolishness.

This is like the use of a mathematical proof being *reductio ad absurdum* (reduced to the absurd). In such a proof, a statement is proved, by assuming its opposite to be true. Logical steps are then taken from this "opposite" argument, until a statement is reached, which can be shown to flow directly and inevitably from the "opposite", and which is absurd.

Perhaps this diagram will help explain.

Suppose we wish to prove statement P. Let P' be the opposite of statement P.

P' => W => X => Y

(P implies W, which implies X, which implies Y)

But Y is obviously absurd.

Therefore, P' is false, which means that P is true.

Here is an example, from math. Yes, you will hate me for introducing math - but, here goes.

Statement to prove: "There is no smallest positive rational number".

We will now propose the opposite, that there exists a number n, which is the smallest possible positive rational number.

Let m = n/2

=> m = ½ . n

However, ½ is a rational number. The product of 2 rationals is a rational. Therefore, m is rational.

However, this is an absurd conclusion, because m < n

Therefore, our original statement "There is no smallest positive rational number" is true.

In our use of Proverbs 26:5, we adopt an entirely similar line of logic. We do not accept the unbeliever's presupposition, but we construct an argument on it nevertheless, to show its absurdity.

For example, an unbeliever might state that "there is no such thing as absolute truth." The Presuppositional Apologist will point out that this statement is an absolute statement.

Another example is when the famous atheist Richard Dawkins suggested that anyone who disagreed with the theory of evolution might be wicked. But the concept of wickedness has no meaning, apart from its definition as being opposite to the character of God - i.e. a biblical concept.

Greg Bahnsen - one of the most quoted Presuppositional Apologists - used an article by the atheistic philosopher Bertrand Russell to illustrate this point. Bahnsen quotes Russell as having advanced three arguments against Christianity, but Bahnsen's application of the principles above is well illustrated by just one of these arguments. Russell's second of his three arguments against Christianity is that there are "serious defects in the character and teaching of Jesus show that he was not the best and wisest of men, but actually morally inferior to Buddha and Socrates."

In response, Bahnsen writes:

Now, if Russell had been reasoning and speaking in terms of the Christian worldview, his attempt to assess moral wisdom, human worthiness, and moral progress—as well as to adversely judge shortcomings in these matters—would be understandable and expected. Christians have a universal, objective and absolute standard of morality in the revealed word of God. But obviously Russell did not mean to be speaking as though he adopted Christian premises and perspectives! On what basis, then, could Russell issue his moral evaluations and judgments? In terms of what view of reality and knowledge did he assume that there was anything like an objective criterion of morality by which to find Christ, Christians, and the church lacking? Russell was embarrassingly arbitrary in this regard. He just took it for granted, as an unargued philosophical bias, that there was a moral standard to apply, and that he could presume to be the spokesman and judge who applies it.[12]

Bahnsen rightly points out that Russell has borrowed the concept of absolute morality from the very Christianity which he seeks to undermine. Not only that, but Russell has taken on himself the mantle of guardian of that morality. He has assumed that his own reason is autonomous, and is superior to those whom he castigates. Once again, we observe the *reductio ad absurdum*, which is the characteristic of our application of Proverbs 26:5.

The reader might, at this point, want more examples of how the use of Proverbs 26:4-5 works out in practice. In my opinion, you could do no better than watch some of the open air preaching of my friend Sye ten Bruggencate. His presentation of the Gospel invariably involves Presuppositional Apologetics in precisely the manner described in this chapter. When I first met Sye, it was notable that we came from very different theological backgrounds, yet had already both developed a foundational commitment to Presuppositional Apologetics. I have no videos of my presentation of these points, plus I am nowhere near as practiced or gifted in the use of this apologetic on the streets. So, I recommend going to his website, take your time to go through the introductory questions, and then head to the multimedia section. As Sye states on his website,

The proof that God exists is that without Him you couldn't prove anything![13]

---

[1] A theist is someone who believes in the existence of gods, whereas a deist is someone whose reason, he supposes, leads him to believe there must be a god

[2] Cosner, Lita (2007), Review of *There is a god*, < http://creation.com/review-there-is-a-god-by-antony-flew >, retrieved 1/11/2016

[3] These sort of schools are called Comprehensive schools in England and in Wales. They are equivalent to what would be called "Public Schools" in the US.

[4] See, for example, 2 Timothy 3:16-17, or 2 Peter 1:20.

[5] Baucham, V. (2015)

[6] Mark 9:40

[7] Luke 11:23

[8] Romans 2:14-15

[9] Proverbs 26:4-5

[10] See, for example, the anonymous *Mennoknight* at < https://mennoknight.wordpress.com/2015/10/22/proverbs-264-5-and-presuppositional-apologetics/ >, retrieved 1/13/2016. Personally, I do not recognize his criticisms as being a genuine reflection of the method suggested by Bahnsen, on which I extemporize here.

[11] I Timothy 6:17-21

[12] Bahnsen, Greg (2011). *Always Ready: Directions for Defending the Faith* (Kindle Locations 2721-2728). . Kindle Edition.

[13] Absolute Apologetics, < http://www.proofthatgodexists.org >, retrieved 1/13/2016

09 Contend Within

A couple of years ago, I spoke at an apologetics conference in San Jose, CA. During one of the essential coffee breaks, I was approached by one of the delegates, holding a book in his hands. My heart sank. I speak at many conferences, and am given many books, pamphlets and papers, by people holding all sorts of weird and wacky ideas that they want to vent in some way. The gentleman was very courteous, as they often are. However, it turned out that the book was not his. And he did not want to spend time riding his own hobby horse. He genuinely wanted to impart a gift, believing that it would be of benefit to all of the speakers at the conference to have a copy. Even so, I put the book into my rucksack and forgot about it. I found it again at the airport, waiting for the plane to fly me back to Pensacola, FL, where I lived at the time.\

The book was called "Biblical Apologetics". I liked the title. Although convinced of the biblical nature of much of Presuppositional Apologetics, I did not want to hold those ideas simply because the ideas formed part of a "system", to which I had subscribed. Moreover, I had already written that I was not keen on referring to myself any more as a "Young Earth Creationist", but preferred the *nom de guerre* "Biblical Creationist".[1] Intrigued, I began to read - and I loved what I read.

The third chapter's title particularly intrigued me. The author, Clifford B McManis, had entitled this "Internal Apologetics".[2] In this chapter, McManis claims that many pastors, eager to get to the apologetic battle with unbelievers, have found themselves more frequently battling to defend the faith against those, who are actually within the church. Having been in innumerable such situations myself, I know from experience that what he writes is true. McManis calls this concept "Internal Apologetics", and claims it is the "Missing In Action" branch of apologetics, being referred to by very few apologists. My first such battle within a church came in my 20s. I wish I had had McManis's book then, or at least had heard of the concept of internal apologetics. A particular doctrinal issue had arisen, on which the pastor was taking a position that was unbiblical. The issue need not be spelled out here, because it is not simple, and the background would take a good deal of space to explain. Nevertheless, a number of us within the church, including most of the senior, biblically minded older Christians, believed that the pastor had the issue wrong. Yet we were, by our own later admission, too reticent. We treated the issue as an intellectual theological discussion, while the pastor and his fans used every logical fallacy in the book, to sway opinions. What no one did was treat the situation as an apologetic situation. Yet, in retrospect, that is what it was. The authority of the Bible was under attack. To cut a long story short, the failure to treat the situation as an apologetic situation rebounded in unexpected ways, devastating a number of families, including that of the pastor, and, indeed, my own.

Contend Earnestly

In one of the least well-known books of the Bible, Jude says:

> *Beloved, although I was very eager to write to you about our common salvation, I found it necessary to write appealing to you to contend for the faith that was once for all delivered to the saints.*[3]

It would appear that Jude had originally wanted to write a doctrinally based epistle, perhaps somewhat similar to Paul's letter to the Romans. However, the Holy Spirit had a different plan, and inspired Jude to write an epistle all about apologetics within the church. Before we examine verse 3 in detail, let's take a look at the next verse, so that we can find out who we are meant to contend against.

> *For certain people have crept in unnoticed who long ago were designated for this condemnation, ungodly people, who pervert the grace of our God into sensuality and deny our only Master and Lord, Jesus Christ.*[4]

The trouble makers, to whom Jude is referring, are not outside the church. They are people who have "crept in unnoticed". Obviously, these people are not real Christians ("designated for this condemnation"). Nevertheless, they appear to be Christians, and are inside the church. This is what McManis refers to as *Internal Apologetics*. Jude is requiring his readers to contend within, as well as without. We will have to jump a little between these two verses, so let's return to verse 3.

If Jude found it necessary to tell his readers to contend for the faith within the church, it would seem to imply that they were not doing so. The Greek word for contend (or "contend earnestly" in some versions) is *epagonizesthai* (επαγωνιζεσθαι). If a Greek word begins with the prefix *epi-*, it often indicates an emphasis on the meaning of the rest of the word; and the I of epi would be ommitted, if follwed by a vowel. Compare this idea with epicenter, epigram etc. So the root word is *agonizesthai*, from which we get our word *agonize*. Have you ever agonized over a family problem? Or, more appropriately, have you evger agonized over a church problem? If you have "extra-agonized", then you have "contended earnestly". That is the level of commitment and action being required by Jude of his readers.

For what is Jude requiring this extra-agonizing contention? He tells us to "contend for the faith". This immediately puts us in mind of 1 Peter 3:15, and yet we are clearly contending within the church. This is certainly internal apologetics in action. The faith for which we contend is "that was once for all delivered to the saints". We are talking about the purity of the Gospel. The issue at stake is not an esoteric disagreement on the finer points of eschatology, nor on intra-church disagreements on seating or singing arrangements. Jude is referring to primary doctrinal disagreements - and these are going on inside the church. As I write this very chapter, I am reminded that a friend of mine posted a comment on Facebook yesterday, bemoaning the fact that, surprisingly, many churches no longer seem to take a clear stance on the subject of the Trinity. Even more shocking, in my opinion, was his observation that even people who claim to hold to the doctrine of the Trinity do not actually care whether other people in their church hold to that teaching or not! The person who denies the Trinity denies either the personhood or the deity (or both) of Jesus Christ. Jude says that such people "pervert the grace of our God". Jude's words are strong, and, because they are under the inspiration of the Holy Spirit, we have to know that these words inform, us what God thinks about the importance of this subject.

I wonder how many Christians have reflected on the impact of Jude 1:5.

> *Now I want to remind you, although you once fully knew it, that Jesus, who saved a people out of the land of Egypt, afterward destroyed those who did not believe.*5

Read that verse several times, and let it sink in. Who saved a people out of Egypt? Well, Moses did, didn't he? But Moses prophesied "The LORD your God will raise up for you a Prophet like me from your midst".[6] Of course, Moses only saved the people out of Egypt, because it was actually God who saved them.

> And the LORD said: "I have surely seen the oppression of My people who are in Egypt, and have heard their cry because of their taskmasters, for I know their sorrows. So I have come down to deliver them out of the hand of the Egyptians, and to bring them up from that land to a good and large land, to a land flowing with milk and honey, to the place of the Canaanites and the Hittites and the Amorites and the Perizzites and the Hivites and the Jebusites.[7]

Does Jude know what he is talking about, when he states that Jesus saved the people out of Egypt? Of course he does; he is writing under inspiration, as we have already stated. Therefore, the logical conclusion is that Jude is saying that Jesus is God, and that Jesus was involved in history, even before his incarnation in Bethlehem. Jude also mentions that this same Jesus, at the time of the Exodus, destroyed Pharaoh and his army in the Red Sea, because of their unbelief. Jude reminds them that they "once fully knew it". Jude wants them fully to know it again, because there is a destruction coming again, for those apostates, who he says have crept into the church, and against whom we should be extra-agonizing - contending within.

These sort of problems are rife in today's churches, even in so-called evangelical, gospel-preaching, Bible-believing churches. The area of apologetics, with which I am most closely associated, is that of creationism. Genesis is the foundational book of the Bible, and the early chapters of Genesis, written in the same historical narrative style as the later chapters, are fundamental to our understanding of the Bible. Yet it is becoming increasingly common for otherwise seemingly sound churches and ministries to undermine the teaching of these chapters. My earlier books on these topics have all been presuppositional in nature.

In 2003, I published my first book, with the title "Just Six Days". This was republished by Master Books in 2007 with the title "The Six Days of Genesis". In that book, I wanted to arrange contemporary creationist thinking in biblical order, as a commentary on the early chapters of Genesis. I did this, to show that we must start from the presupposition that the Bible is true. This is what I said, in the first chapter of that book>

> *The question in a study such as this is always "Where shall we start our study?" I used to start by tackling the science, showing that evolution is wrong. More recently, I have come*

to the view that the main problem in today's church is a lack
of belief in the bible itself, so I now tend to start from the
Bible's account and build the argument from there.[8]

In 2010, I published a book called "Itching Ears", in which I showed that every doctrine of Christianity is found reflected or founded in the early chapters of Genesis. This is an important point, because too many modern evangelical theologians seem to be given a pass on their views on Genesis. We like what they say on New Testament topics, so we recommend people to read them, even though we know that their well-publicized views on Genesis are in error. I made this point, in the chapter on "The Inerrancy of Scripture".

Paul commends Timothy for knowing the scriptures. He
describes these scriptures as "holy" - which means "set apart"
- literally, set apart for God. Paul tells Timothy that the
Scriptures are there to make him wise. So his wisdom is not to
come from external sources, but only to be based on
scripture.[9]

"Don't Miss the Boat" (2013) was all about the Flood. In that book, also, I notice that I commented early on an apologetic theme.

Regrettably, so-called conservative evangelical churches have led the way, in recent years, in compiling a theology of doubt.[10]

And, if I may be permitted one more self-quote, in 2015, my book "Where Birds Eat Horses" attempts to show non-scientific Christians how they can spot true and false presuppositions in scientific articles and media.

Many creationists have been asked for evidence that creation happened as it says in the Bible, or evidence that the Bible is true. They have requested that this evidence be neutral. Now, I have a presupposition that God exists and that the Bible is true. Therefore, I interpret every piece of evidence through this filter. In a radio discussion program on BBC radio some years ago, Richard Dawkins said of me "every point this man makes, he always quotes the Bible." It was not meant as a compliment, but I took it as one. The point that so many, including so many Christians, fail to understand is that everyone has a presupposition. In order to find step off my presupposition that the Bible is true, I have to adopt a line of reasoning, into which the Bible is not relevant. This is not a neutral position at all. It is a highly presuppositional position.[11]

All of these books are filed under Creationism, or maybe Creation Science. But I saw each of them as being there to defend the faith. The fact remains that much of the intended audience, who I want to challenge, is inside the church, rather than outside of it.

Jude is not alone in urging the defence of the faith inside the church. Paul does likewise. In his second letter to Timothy, he gives the following instructions to the younger preacher.

> *I charge you in the presence of God and of Christ Jesus, who is to judge the living and the dead, and by his appearing and his kingdom: preach the word; be ready in season and out of season; reprove, rebuke, and exhort, with complete patience and teaching.*[12]

Notice that the instruction to Timothy is to preach the word. It ought not to be necessary to comment on this, but it has become so common for churches to place less of an emphasis on preaching the word. Some churches are happy to abandon a sermon, if "the worship is going well" - forgetting that the preaching is actually part of the worship. But even those churches where the sermon is not missed, the teaching diet can be skinny, involving endless topical sermons, instead of biblical exposition. Don't misunderstand this last comment. It can be very helpful for a preacher occasionally to pick up on a topic, and explain it from Scripture. But this should not be the norm. The norm should be the exposition of God's word, because that is where our doctrines should actually be from. Paul continues:

> For the time is coming when people will not endure sound teaching, but having itching ears they will accumulate for themselves teachers to suit their own passions, and will turn away from listening to the truth and wander off into myths.[3]

It is truly frightening to contemplate how much that 1st century sentence exactly matches what is happening in so many 21st century churches. Like Jude, Paul is concerned about those within the church, who are leading folks away to other doctrines. These doctrines are "to suit their own passions". What do we have, if we don't have a Scriptural foundation? We have "myths". As soon as we have myths, we have no way of determining whose myth is valid and whose isn't. All we have are opinions. A new opinion can come along at any time. Paul, like Jude, wants his people grounded in the solid foundation, the presupposition of the truth of God's word.

---

[1] More on the reasons for this later

[2] McManis, C.B. (2013), *Biblical Apologetics*, (Xlibris), location 1114 (this refers to the Kindle edition, although I originally read the paperback)

[3] Jude 1:3 (ESV)

[4] Jude 1:4 (ESV)

[5] Jude 1:5 (ESV)

[6] Deuteronomy 18:15

[7] Exodus 3:7-8

[8] Taylor, P.F. (2007), *The Six Days of Genesis*, (Master Books), p17

[9] Taylor, P.F. (2010), *Itching Ears*, (J6D Publications), p132

[10] Taylor, P.F. (2013), *Don't Miss the Boat*, (Master Books), p7

[11] Taylor, P.F. (2015), *Where Birds Eat Horses*, (J6D Publications), p51

[12] 2 Timothy 4:1-2 (ESV)

[13] 2 Timothy 4:3-4 (ESV)

10 Where the Evidence Leads

We have already seen that a common refrain of the Classical Apologist is to "see where the evidence leads", with the idea that it is evidence that will lead people independently to a knowledge of God. In this book, however, we have seen that this is a mistaken approach, not sanctioned by Scripture. Even if such an approach were to bring someone to the knowledge that there exists some form of higher creator, this being does not have the attributes of the true God of the Bible, and is therefore a false god - an idol.

My constant criticism of such a concept, therefore, might lead one to suppose that evidence should never be used under any circumstances. This is, in fact, not the case. It is completely justifiable to use evidence. It is simply that the evidence is not there to attempt to prove the existence if God. But within a Presuppositional Apologetic, there is most definitely a place for the correct use of evidence. This correct use of evidence is what we must now explore. We will undertake this exploration, by starting with the use of evidence by Jesus, and, in particular, his post-resurrection encounter with the apostle Thomas.

Thomas wanted evidence in order to believe that Jesus had risen from the dead.

Now Thomas, called the Twin, one of the twelve, was not with them when Jesus came. The other disciples therefore said to him, "We have seen the Lord." So he said to them, "Unless I see in His hands the print of the nails, and put my finger into the print of the nails, and put my hand into His side, I will not believe."[1]

Thomas laid out the very clear criteria that he required in order to believe that Jesus had indeed risen. When he was confronted by Jesus, however, his reaction was dramatically different.

And after eight days His disciples were again inside, and Thomas with them. Jesus came, the doors being shut, and stood in the midst, and said, "Peace to you!" Then He said to Thomas, "Reach your finger here, and look at My hands; and reach your hand here, and put it into My side. Do not be unbelieving, but believing." And Thomas answered and said to Him, "My Lord and my God!"[2]

Thomas believed, when he finally met with Jesus—albeit later than he really should have believed! He believed, because he had met with Jesus, not because of the evidence. In the same way, we should call on people to believe, regardless of the evidence. Belief is the result of meeting with Jesus.

Does that mean that evidence is not required? Not necessarily. In the above account, we find that Thomas actually is provided with the evidence that he sought, despite his declaration of worship to Jesus. Jesus offered Thomas the opportunity to experience the evidence, exactly as Thomas had originally requested. Why did Jesus do this? We find out in the next verse.

> *Jesus said to him, "Thomas, because you have seen Me,*
> *you have believed. Blessed are those who have not seen and*
> *yet have believed."*[3]

Jesus provides the evidence, in order to emphasize again to Thomas that the evidence is not needed. The very existence of **Jesus as revealed in Scripture** is enough for our faith. So the offer of evidence to Thomas was not in order to prove what Thomas had earlier wanted to know, but rather as a rebuke for Thomas, and as a teaching strategy on the correct use of evidence. The evidence only makes sense in the light of Thomas's late declaration, that Jesus was his Lord and his God. Jesus emphasizes that there would be more blessing for those who believed without this request for evidence. This correct context for the use of evidence will be further analyzed below.

The Nature of Scientific Theory

Both creationists and evolutionists make mistakes over the use of the term "scientific theory". The sort of creationists who make this mistake are usually well-meaning individuals, who want to make a valid point, but who do not have the benefit of a university scientific education. However, the misuse of the term "theory" by evolutionists is usually done for bait-and-switch purposes, in the full knowledge that they are illogically mixing differing definitions, in order to win an argument.

The mistaken comment used by amateur creationists is this; "evolution is just a theory." This statement is used, because it is thought, mistakenly, that a theory is a lower standard of scientific methodology than a scientific law. Evolutionists rightly pounce on this naïve comment, by pointing out the difference between scientific theory and law. These definitions, with which I concur, come from the National Academy of Sciences (NAS).

Terms Used in Describing the Nature of Science

Fact: In science, an observation that has been repeatedly confirmed and for all practical purposes is accepted as "true." Truth in science, however, is never final, and what is accepted as a fact today may be modified or even discarded tomorrow.

Hypothesis: A tentative statement about the natural world leading to deductions that can be tested. If the deductions are verified, it becomes more probable that the hypothesis is correct. If the deductions are incorrect, the original hypothesis can be abandoned or modified. Hypotheses can be used to build more complex inferences and explanations.

Law: A descriptive generalization about how some aspect of the natural world behaves under stated circumstances.

Theory: In science, a well-substantiated explanation of some aspect of the natural world that can incorporate facts, laws, inferences, and tested hypotheses.[4]

So, if a creationist states that "evolution is just a theory," he is implying that it is not yet a law, because he is making the error that a theory, when sufficiently substantiated, will become a law. The NAS quote continues:

The contention that evolution should be taught as a "theory, not as a fact" confuses the common use of these words with the scientific use. In science, theories do not turn into facts through the accumulation of evidence. Rather, theories are the end points of science. They are understandings that develop from extensive observation, experimentation, and creative reflection. They incorporate a large body of scientific facts, laws, tested hypotheses, and logical inferences. In this sense, evolution is one of the strongest and most useful scientific theories we have.[5]

While taking this criticism on the chin, we will have some important things to say about the last sentence of that quote in a moment.

The NAS quote acknowledges that there is a difference between common uses of the words "theory" and "law" and their scientific uses. The atheist website, Rational Wiki, picks up on this point in its article on Scientific Theory.

Another common misconception is that a theory is the step you go through while on your way to a law of science. Scientific laws and theories are two very different things and, despite what it may seem, one never becomes the other. Scientific laws are factual observations usually derived from mathematical modeling; they merely distill empirical results into concise verbal or mathematical statements that express a fundamental principle of science—for example, gravity attracts, force equals mass times acceleration and so on. Theories are the causal explanations behind what creates these laws and observations of nature.[6]

The deliberate confusion of the common use of the word "theory" with the scientific use of the term would therefore be a logical fallacy. Now consider the following comment from the late Dr. Richard Pike, former Chief Executive of the Royal Society of Chemistry, in a document criticizing any attempt to teach creation in science lessons in British comprehensive schools (which would be referred to as "public schools" in the USA).

> *Above all, we should no longer talk of the theory of evolution as though it is 'just an idea.' So well-established is it, that it now warrants the designation of an immutable scientific law, and should be taught as such.*[7]

Pike's suggestion here is that a theory has a lower level of factual basis than a law. This is precisely what the NAS document was explaining is NOT the case. Dr. Richard Pike was one of Britain's most eminent scientists. There is no suggestion in my mind that he was ignorant of the correct scientific definitions of these terms. That he should use the terms for theory and law in this *common* manner, rather than the *scientific* manner, in a submission to British Government officials who are not noted for their scientific literacy, must have been done on purpose. Rational Wiki defines the logical fallacy known as equivocation thus:

> **Equivocation** *is a logical fallacy that relies on the different meanings a word can have in different contexts.*[8]

One writer has been refreshingly honest about the reasons for this use of logical fallacies.

> *Let's be honest: debate is not just about finding truth, it's also about winning. If you think a fallacious argument can slide by and persuade the judge to vote for you, you're going to make it, right? The trick is not getting caught.*[9]

In a similar definition to that of the NAS, used for the same purpose of criticizing creationism, the American Association for the Advancement of Science defines a scientific theory as:

> *A well-substantiated explanation of some aspect of the natural world, based on a body of facts that have been repeatedly confirmed through observation and experiment.*[10]

In what universe has molecules-to-man evolution ever been observed? The best we can say for alleged human evolution, for example, is that it has been *inferred* from fossil evidence, in accordance with evolutionary presuppositions. It has not been *observed* to happen. The weakness of that aspect of defining evolution as a theory can clearly be seen, even before we challenge the logical basis of the inference. And in what laboratory has any experiment been performed, which gives evidence for evolution? The answer is none.

With this in mind, we see clearly that the amateur creationist argument that "evolution is just a theory" is somewhat wide of the mark. It would be more correct to say, in the light of the correct scientific definition of the word *theory*, that "evolution is not even a theory."

One important feature of a scientific theory is that it is capable of falsification. It is, however, never capable of being absolutely proved. In supporting this aspect of what a theory is, Helmenstine has said:

A theory is valid as long as there is no evidence to dispute it ... Example: It is known that on June 30, 1908 in Tunguska, Siberia, there was an explosion equivalent to the detonation of about 15 million tons of TNT. Many hypotheses have been proposed for what caused the explosion. It is theorized that the explosion was caused by a natural extraterrestrial phenomenon, and was not caused by man. Is this theory a fact? No. The event is a recorded fact. Is this theory generally accepted to be true, based on evidence to-date? Yes. Can this theory be shown to be false and be discarded? Yes.[11]

This is how the testing of a theory should work.

• Theory A seems to fit observations B

• Observation C is contrary to what is predicted by Theory A

• Therefore, Theory A should be rejected.

In practice, however, a great deal of intellectual capital has been invested in the development of highly sophisticated, but errant, evolutionary theories. Therefore the theories are not discarded, but rather rescuing devices are devised to amend the theory, in order to take into account the new "problem". Thus, evolutionary theories—such as Darwin's Theory of Evolution, or the Big Bang Theory—begin to resemble student automobiles, which are frequently held together with string and duct tape! I have often considered what might happen if an expedition to a remote part of the world found and captured a live dinosaur. For example, if the accounts of *Mkele Mwembi*, a sauropod alleged to live in the upper reaches of Africa's Congo River, are true, and if one were found and captured, and shipped to a large American zoo and put on display, would this cause the theory of evolution to be overturned? In my opinion, the answer would be "No." Instead, evolutionists would find rescuing mechanisms that would "explain" why this dinosaur alone had survived the 65 million years or so since that meteorite was supposed to have wiped out the dinosaurs. That is because evolution is not a theory; it is a religion, or philosophy. For many, it is a way of life.

Evidence and Faith

Many atheists have criticized the concept of faith. They see faith as something somewhat nebulous. The accusation is that Christians believe in "the magic man in the sky." They wish to equate the Christians' belief in God with concepts such as the Tooth Fairy, the Easter Bunny or Santa Claus.

One atheist has commented:

There's an equal amount of evidence for the existence of all of the above [God, Santa, Tooth Fairy].

The importance of God does not give weight to His existence. It gives weight to the question of His existence. If

He exists, that's important. If He doesn't exist, that's
important. If a god besides Him exists, that's just as
important. This importance doesn't count as evidence one
way or another.

The comparison to Santa Claus, the Tooth Fairy etcetera is
meant to highlight the similarity in evidence levels between
entities we all immediately dismiss as false and entities some
people hold truer than anything. It's a tool for establishing
perspective.

The equation of God and imaginary beliefs like the Tooth
Fairy require two assumptions on the part of the atheist.

1. Faith requires evidence

2. Faith can be defined as a lack of evidence

Neither of these assumptions really makes sense. Let's see
them in action in the words of one very well-known atheist, Dr.
Richard Dawkins.

People like to say that faith and science can live together,
side by side. But I don't think they can. Science is a discipline
of investigation and constructive doubt. Faith demands a
positive suspension of critical faculties.[12]

I agree with Dawkins that science involves "investigation
and constructive doubt." If scientific investigation is to be

conducted well, the investigator has to be prepared to try to falsify hypotheses that are being tested. However, there is no evidence that "faith demands a positive suspension of critical faculties." Dawkins has made similar comments before. In his book, *The Selfish Gene*, he states:

> *Faith means blind trust, in the absence of evidence, even in the teeth of evidence.*[13]

Dawkins is adamant that faith and evidence are to be seen as opposites or, at least, incompatible. Yet his statement bears no relationship to the facts. Many pioneering scientists of the modern era were people of faith. One thinks of such names as Newton, Pasteur, Lister, Priestley, Kelvin and Faraday. It is fun to think of Dawkins in a time machine having the effrontery to accuse these giants of science of flying in the "teeth of evidence." It is interesting that Dawkins' commitment to evidence does not always remain so strong. For example, when asked to give evidence for his intellectual commitment to Darwinian evolution as the explanation of human origins, he said:

> *We don't need evidence. We know it to be true.*

The author and apologist C.S. Lewis (famous for his *Chronicles of Narnia*) had a more mature view of the relationship between faith and evidence.

I believe in Christianity as I believe that the sun has risen. Not only because I see it, but because by it I see everything else.[14]

Lewis is not usually thought of as a presuppositional apologist. Nevertheless, he has understood the issue. Seeing the sun is looking at the evidence. However, Lewis sees everything else, because of the sun. Similarly, evidence is not neutral. All evidence is interpreted in the light of our presupposition of the existence of God and truth of the Bible. That is why the writer to the Hebrews says this:

Now faith is the substance of things hoped for, the evidence of things not seen. For by it the elders obtained a good testimony. By faith we understand that the worlds were framed by the word of God, so that the things which are seen were not made of things which are visible.[15]

We notice from these verses that our *knowledge* of origins comes from faith, because the writer says "by faith we understand ..." Faith is therefore substantial. Indeed, although it is difficult for those without faith to understand this point, Hebrews 11:1 tells us that our faith does not require evidence—our faith **is** the evidence. The search for more evidence to prove the truth of our faith is therefore counterproductive. The evidence means nothing without its interpretation in the light of our presupposition of faith.

Evidence and the Authority of Scripture

The arguments above lead me to my main objection to what I consider to be incorrect uses of evidential apologetics. Those who propose the use of evidence to "prove" the Bible are well-meaning. Their concern is their own high view of Scripture. I have indulged in such evidential apologetics myself for many years because I wanted people to trust the Bible. Yet my very attempts to prove the Bible actually undermine the Bible! How can this be? Let me explain.

On page 112, I referred to a student being taught about atoms. She had difficulty believing the atomic model. What could I do to persuade her? I couldn't get a microscope out and let her see inside the atom, because that is not possible. In fact, what I usually did in such circumstances is show a student the relevant pages in a text book.

Having seen the text book, she now accepted the standard atomic model. Which source of information had the higher authority for her? Was it me, as her teacher, or the text book? It is clearly the text book, because it was the text book that convinced her that what I said was correct.

Now suppose that I could find a piece of evidence, which will call Evidence E. I use Evidence E to convince someone that the Bible is true. For that person, which evidence has the higher authority? Is it the Bible, or is it Evidence E? Clearly, it is Evidence E that proves the Bible to be true.

However, the Bible claims to be the highest possible authority. Yet, in this example, it does not have as high an authority as Evidence E. Therefore, Evidence E has not actually proved the Bible to be true. The very existence of Evidence E disproves the idea that the Bible is the highest authority. Therefore, the proof of the Bible by the use of Evidence E is literally self-refuting.

This misuse of evidence is seen in a number of classic creationist arguments. For example, many have suggested that the definition of Young Earth Creationism is the belief that the world is no more than 10,000 years old. But where does that number come from? If, like Archbishop Ussher, one calculates the age of the earth, one finds it to be about 6,000 years old. The date of 10,000 years comes, in fact, from a number of limiting pieces of scientific evidence which are consistent with a "young" age for the earth. The point is this: Do we accept a "young" age for the earth because of certain scientific evidence, or do we accept the biblical age, because it is from the Bible. The latter should be our reason for believing, not the former. Although the idea that, for example, the break-up of comets is incompatible with an earthly age of greater than 10,000 years, it is not for this reason that we accept such a timescale. The truth of the Bible is always to be our presupposition.

Good Use of Evidence

In view of all that I have written above, it would seem as if I am arguing that evidence should not be used, because it undermines Scripture. That is not the case. I have simply said that the attempt to use evidence to prove the Bible undermines the authority of Scripture. There are, however, ways of using evidence which are both legitimate and effective. All of these methods involve evidence in its proper context; interpreted in the light of our presupposition of the truth of Scripture, not used as a spurious "proof" of Scripture.

One creation speaker who has written and spoken a great deal on the subject of presuppositional apologetics is the astrophysicist Dr. Jason Lisle. In his important book, *The Ultimate Proof of Creation*, he suggests that there are four good reasons for using evidence in a presuppositional context. He gives these as:

- Confirming Biblical Creation

- An Introduction to Worldviews

- Showing Inconsistency and Arbitrariness

- Preconditions of Intelligibility[16]

Confirming Biblical Creation

Lisle is not suggesting that evidence proves creation. He is suggesting that evidence is consistent with the biblical account of creation. Lisle says "Many evolutionists conflate 'science' with 'evolution', hoping that they can convince people that we must accept evolution if we are going to accept science. Such erroneous teachings must be challenged, and scientific evidence is very useful in accomplishing this." It is therefore useful for us to give good scientific evidences, having stated our presupposition. Some people accuse creationists of circular arguments when they do this. However, that is an incorrect use of the definition of circular argument. A genuinely fallacious circular argument is when the outcome is assumed at the outset, but this fact is not admitted. The creationist, on the other hand, is open and honest about his presupposition.

We stated earlier that there were no creationist fossils or evolutionary fossils—only fossils. So we do not offer fossils, for example, as proof that the Flood of Genesis 6–8 actually occurred. However, given our commitment to biblical truth, and therefore armed with the knowledge that the Genesis Flood actually occurred, it is completely reasonable to state what sort of fossilization we would expect, and to present the evidence in the context that this fossil evidence is to be expected from our presupposition.

An Introduction to Worldviews

One of the most important facts that we need to communicate is this issue that everyone begins with presuppositions. The evolutionist, however, frequently does not realize that he has presuppositions. Therefore, the use of evidence, together with the ability to interpret that evidence in different ways, is important to illustrate this fact. The fallacy of the evolutionist is the belief that evidence speaks for itself. We need to show that evidence says nothing by itself, but is interpreted according to worldviews.

Showing Inconsistency and Arbitrariness

The use of evidence by evolutionists is frequently both inconsistent and arbitrary. Examples have already been given in this ebook, such as the confusion by evolutionists over the use of the term *scientific theory*, even as they accuse creationists of similar confusion.

A good example of such arbitrariness is the difference in standard between scientists looking for intelligible messages from space (SETI) while refusing to accept evidence for intelligence in DNA. SETI has devised many tests to see whether signals from other stars contain code that can only represent language and intelligence. These boxes are all checked by the code inherently present in DNA. But the arbitrariness is that different scientists will use different standards in these different circumstances, because of their preconceptions and presuppositions in both areas.

Preconditions of Intelligibility

In the previous paragraphs, we have seen that we can educate our opponents to understand that their worldview affects their interpretation of evidence. Under this heading, we show our opponents that the different worldviews are not equally valid. We have often stated at Creation Today that "without God, it is impossible to know anything." Similarly, without the truth of the Bible it is impossible to prove anything, as we need a true baseline, from which we can judge things.

The practice of science requires the existence of absolutes. If this were not so, there could be no peer-review of experimental results, because if results differed from day to day, even if the conditions were the same, we would not be able to state anything meaningful about those results. Yet the atheistic evolutionary worldview cannot account for the existence of scientific absolutes—or absolutes in the fields of logic or morality. Dawkins, for example, has compared the teaching of creationism to children as "wicked." However, the term "wicked" is a moral term that has no place in his worldview. Therefore, his use of the term is illogical. If, for example, it could be shown that a nation might prosper by lying to its people that creationism is true, then surely, in evolutionary terms of the survival of the fittest, such a lie would be acceptable. Of course, I do not accept that the statement that "creationism is true" is a lie. I am merely using

Dawkins' own logic, to show that his very opposition to God is only possible logically if God exists, and his appeal to morality is nonsensical, as morality has no logical basis in his worldview.

Use of Evidence

One creationist, who had taken issue with the presuppositional approach, had these points carefully explained to him. His response was "you do it your way, and I'll do it my way." Unfortunately, by saying this, he had missed the point, because his over-emphasis on evidential apologetics undermined his proclamation of the truth of the Bible and therefore the Gospel itself.

With this in mind, we continue to use evidence and continue to collect evidence, but we use evidence only in its correct presuppositional context. It is only in that context that it can be used to glorify God. We must be careful and appropriate as creationists in how we defend the truth. If we defend the correct truth, with an incorrect argument, we bring the truth into disrepute. So this ebook is a call for creationist integrity. We have the truth, because it has been revealed to us by God in His word. Now let's proclaim that truth in a way that honors Him.

[1] John 20:24-25

[2] John 20:26-28

[3] John 20:29

[4] Teaching About Evolution and the Nature of Science by the National Academy of Sciences (Washington, D.C.: National Academy Press, 1998).

[5] *ibid*

[6] Scientific Theory, Rational Wiki, < http://rationalwiki.org/wiki/Scientific_theory >, retrieved 1/14/2016

[7] Pike, R. (2007), Teach All Eleven Year Olds the Law of Evolution, Royal Society of Chemistry, < http://www.rsc.org/images/EvolutionRichardPike_tcm18-52757.pdf >, retrieved 1/14/2016

[8] Equivocation, Rational Wiki, < http://rationalwiki.org/wiki/Equivocation >, retrieved 1/14/2016

[9] Logical Fallacies and the Art of Debate, < http://www.csun.edu/~dgw61315/fallacies.html >, retrieved 1/14/2016

[10] Science and Creationism: A View from the National Academy of Sciences, Second Edition (1999) , Introduction

[11] Helmenstine, A.M., Scientific Hypothesis, Theory, Law Definitions,

< http://chemistry.about.com/od/chemistry101/a/lawtheory. htm >, retrieved 1/14/2016

[12] Dawkins, R. *The Root of All Evil*, Channel 4 Television Documentary (UK)

[13] Dawkins, R. *The Selfish Gene,* (London: Paladin/Granada, 1978), p212.

[14] Lewis, C.S. (1945), "Is Theology Poetry?", Included in *The Weight of Glory*, a collection of letters and articles, (HarperOne: 2001)

[15] Hebrews 11:1-3

[16] Lisle, J. (2009), *The Ultimate Proof of Creation*, (Master Books)

11 Reason and the Sovereignty of God

The title is there for a reason (yes, that is deliberate). There are many people who wish to say that we must give up our reason, if we want to follow a Presuppositional Apologetic. They would state that this is because we substitute an overriding commitment to the doctrine of the Sovereignty of God over the ability to use our brains.

Moreover, there are others who would oppose Presuppositional Apologetics, because of its frequent association with Reformed theology. Now, this chapter is not the time or the place to discuss the merits or otherwise of Reformed theology. It is not that I do not want to discuss that argument. I will happily discuss it elsewhere. It is simply that I do not think it is relevant to the acceptance of Presuppositional Apologetics. It is my contention that Presuppositional Apologetics is the correct and biblical way to defend the faith, because of a high view of the Sovereignty of God. One might argue that this is a circular argument, that I presuppose that God exists and the Bible is true, because I presuppose that the God of the Bible is Sovereign. But not every circular argument is invalid. If the circular argument contains the important presupposition, on which all your logical arguments are based, then I suggest that it is a non-vicious circle.

This is an important point, in view of the difficulties that so many Christians seem to have with this apologetic. One critical article, that seems to represent some of these difficulties, was published by a Christian.

> *One cannot start epistemologically outside of the self. The presuppositionalists' solution to the brain in the vat problem is their testimony of the triune God of Scripture. They have started with God epistemologically, and from there, everything else happens to fall into place. This is to be contrasted against the non-believer, who starts with their own reasoning and their own mind, which leaves them unable to solve the brain in the vat problem. Of course, as the title of this subsection indicated, a person cannot epistemologically begin outside of the self. It is a limitation of the human experience.*[1]

The key errant phrase is this: "a person cannot epistemologically begin outside of the self". To this statement, one has to respond "Why not?" There is no logical reason why our epistemology should not begin outside of oneself, other than that does not seem to be this person's experience. Yet his experience is, I submit, irrelevant, because the Bible has told us otherwise. The Bible has very clearly told us that "the fear of the Lord is the beginning of knowledge."[2] Indeed, his argument is much akin to the old earth theologian, who claims that there is a 67th book of the Bible, the book of nature, and that we must re-interpret the Bible if these appear to disagree. It is no surprise, therefore, to find that this critic of Presuppositional Apologetics does indeed believe the 67th book approach.

> As such, if we find something in nature that contradicts the Bible, if we find some real science or real evidence that contradicts the Bible, the question is what we have misunderstood. If we find that we understand the Bible properly, then we need to take another look at the science. If we find that we understand the science properly, then we need to take another look at the Bible. We need to reinterpret the Bible to accommodate real science. Both the natural world and Scripture are from God, so it would be a mistake to say that one is right and the other is wrong. If we were to say that science is wrong and not valuable, then we are saying that we cannot learn anything about the universe through investigation, which would be patently flawed, considering the success of scientific naturalism and the flourishing of technology in this era.[3]

In the same manner as above, this author has made assertions, which are incorrect. He has suggested that there might be real science or real evidence that contradicts the Bible. But, as we have seen, evidence is always interpreted by a person's worldview. He forgets that there is no contemporary laboratory experiment that can be done to measure the age of rocks. The age of a rock is calculated, according to a number of presuppositions, however sophisticated these presuppositions may appear. This author does not have a time machine for direct measurement, So there is no real science that contradicts the Bible. Rather, it is incumbent on us to start from the truth of the Bible, and interpret the evidence in the light of that presupposition. And when this author comments that the natural world is "from God", he forgets that because of the fall we are able to make mistakes in examining evidences of the natural world.

Reasoning from the Scriptures

There is most definitely a place for reasoning within this apologetic. Indeed, perhaps reasoning only becomes logical, when one's presuppositions are acknowledged.
That is why our proof of God includes the necessary corollary that any of any other presupposition is illogical, or absurd.

In Acts 17, we have the apostle Paul's masterly presentation and defense of the Gospel. But, in order to understand what is happening at Mars Hill, we need to understand the context of Paul's presentation. Acts 17 actually begins with Paul in Thessalonica.

Then Paul, as his custom was, went in to them, and for three Sabbaths reasoned with them from the Scriptures,

*explaining and demonstrating that the Christ had to suffer
and rise again from the dead, and saying, "This Jesus whom I
preach to you is the Christ."*[4]

Paul's first port of call is the synagogue. What does he start
to do? He reasons with them. But notice that he reasons with
them "from the Scriptures". This a reasoning of logic, as well
as exposition. But it all stems from the Scriptures. Luke tells us
that this was his custom.

So, when Paul was forced to leave Thessalonica, we would
expect to see him following the same custom in Athens. And
that is indeed what we find.

*Therefore he reasoned in the synagogue with the Jews and
with the Gentile worshipers, and in the marketplace daily
with those who happened to be there.*[5]

Once again, Paul is using reason. We must assume he is
following the same custom as before, so it makes sense to
assume that he is reasoning from the Scriptures - even with
those in the marketplace. And this latter point would seem to
be correct, because the Epicurean and Stoic philosophers
accuse him of advocating foreign gods - Jesus and the
resurrection.[6] Finally, when Paul stands at Mars Hill
(Areopagus), he gives a speech, in which he does not directly
quote from Scripture. Nevertheless, he alludes to biblical ideas

throughout, including an insistence on creation, which would have been alien to his Greek listeners. Some have used Paul's Mars Hill speech as an example against Presuppositional Apologetics, because he quotes Greek poetry. However, it will be noticed that, of all the poetry he could have quoted, he deliberately chooses lines which are in agreement with the Bible. His careful choice, even of non-biblical poetry, indicates his presuppositional commitment to the authority of Scripture.

Reasoning with the Scriptures

The use of logical reasoning is important, even in the interpretation or application of Scriptures. "But surely God is higher than logic", some might object. That may well be true, but God, being perfect, is logical. Some have suggested that aspects of God's nature - the Trinity, for example - are illogical. That is not so. There is nothing illogical about the Trinity. It is certainly a difficult concept to grasp, but that does not make it illogical.

Jason Lisle comments further on this, in his book, *Understanding Genesis*.

> *God expects us to use logic and draw proper conclusions from the text of Scripture. In fact, you cannot know that you are saved without using logic. Here's why. The Bible nowhere states, "Dr. Lisle is saved." Instead it states, "If you confess with your mouth Jesus as Lord, and believe in your heart that God raised Him from the dead, you will be saved" (Romans 10:*

9). Furthermore, I know that I have confessed with my mouth that Jesus is Lord, and I have believed in my heart that God raised Him from the dead. I conclude logically that I am saved.[7]

Perhaps it might be reading too much into Isaiah 1 to see the same principle at work. However, God is appealing to his people to use reason, based on their knowledge of Him, and their knowledge of their own sin.

"Come now, and let us reason together," Says the LORD, "Though your sins are like scarlet, They shall be as white as snow; Though they are red like crimson, They shall be as wool.[8]

Lisle argues that all interpretation of Scripture should be logical. He describes this as a rule of hermeneutics. Hermeneutics is that discipline, in which portions of the Bible are interpreted, according to their literary style. For example, the poetry in Psalms is not interpreted in the same way as the narrative history of Genesis. Once again, this is governed by logic.

The most important rule of hermeneutics is that you should have an objective reason for your interpretation. The second most important rule is that the reason must be good (self-consistent, not violating rules of logic, etc.). All the other rules simply flesh out these two.[9]

In many ways, Lisle is arguing for common sense. When we read that Jesus said "Love your neighbor..." we do not suppose He actually meant "Throw fluffy teddy bears in the air". Yet this seems to be how many people approach their apologetics, arguing, for example, that when God said He made the world in six days, using constructions which everywhere else in the Bible would imply six literal 24-hour days, we, as human interpreters, are somehow allowed to tell God what He actually meant. It might not make sense to you, at first, that the Bible means what it says. But that does not make it illogical. It is far more logical to start with the truth of God's word, and see where that takes you.

---

[1] Bushey, R. (2015), *Against Presuppositional Apologetics,* < http://thereforegodexists.com/against-presuppositional-apologetics/ >, retrieved 1/15/2016

[2] Proverbs 1:7

[3] Bushey, R. (2015), *Is It Okay To Reinterpret Scripture To Accommodate Modern Science?,* < http://thereforegodexists.com/is-it-okay-to-reinterpret-scripture-to-accommodate-modern-science/ >, retrieved 1/15/2016

4 Acts 17:2-3

5 Acts 17:17

6 As the Greek word for resurrection is *anastasis* (αναστασιν), which sounds like a female Greek name, many have suggested that they misunderstood Paul, and thought he was referring to a male and female deity couple. This is possible, but I have footnoted it, rather than included it in the text, because I think the point is not relevant to my central argument

7 Lisle, J. (2015). Understanding Genesis: How to Analyze, Interpret, and Defend Scripture (Kindle Locations 2574-2577). Master Books. Kindle Edition.

8 Isaiah 1:18

9 Lisle, J. (2015). Understanding Genesis: How to Analyze, Interpret, and Defend Scripture (Kindle Locations 2661-2663). Master Books. Kindle Edition.

12 Defend from the Start

"Where did you first get the idea of Presuppositional Apologetics from?", I am often asked. "Was it from van Till, or Greg Bahnsen? Perhaps it was from Gordon Clark. Maybe it was from Jason Lisle or Sye ten Bruggencate."

No. None of the above. I came into contact with Presuppositional Apologetics through the writings of Ken Ham. Now, most of you reading this probably do not recognize Ken as an advocate of presuppositional apologetics. The reason for that is that he rarely uses that term. But I learned from his writing and his presentations the methodology that I later realized was Presuppositional Apologetics. Ken refers to the presuppositions as "starting points".

Just visit the Answers in Genesis Creation Museum, in northern Kentucky, and you will see this in action. After the initial information boards, you arrive at a display, showing a dinosaur dig. Two palaeontologists are studying it. They are working together, on the same fossil, at the same dig, but they come up with different conclusions about how the dinosaur fossil get there. The reason for this is made clear in the exhibition - they have different starting points, different presuppositions.

Presuppositional Creationism
Ken explains this philosophy thus:

Over the past several years, some so-called evidence for creation has been shown not to be reliable. Some of these are

- *supposed human and dinosaur footprints found together at the Paluxy River in Texas;*

- *the small accumulation of moon dust found by the Apollo astronauts;*

- *a boat-like structure in the Ararat region as evidence of Noah's ark;*

- *a supposed human handprint found in "dinosaur-age rock";*

- *a dead "plesiosaur" caught near New Zealand.*

Most well-meaning, informed creationists would agree in principle that things which are not carefully documented and researched should not be used. But in practice, many of them are very quick to accept the sorts of facts mentioned here, without asking too many questions. They are less cautious than they might otherwise be, because they are so keen to have "our" facts/evidences to counter "theirs." What they really don't understand, however, is that it's not a matter of "their facts vs. ours." All facts are actually interpreted, and all scientists actually have the same observations—the same data—available to them.

Creationists and evolutionists, Christians and non-Christians, all have the same facts. Think about it: we all have the same earth, the same fossil layers, the same animals and plants, the same stars—the facts are all the same.

The difference is in the way we all interpret the facts. And why do we interpret facts differently? Because we start with different presuppositions; these are things that are assumed to be true without being able to prove them. These then become the basis for other conclusions. All reasoning is based on presuppositions (also called axioms). This becomes especially relevant when dealing with past events.[1]

I heard Ken give this explanation in a talk, many years before the publication of the book, from which I have extensively quoted (and, to which I was a contributor). I was blown away by it. I had been making precisely those mistakes in my creationist presentations. In order to counteract evolution, I offered evidence. I remember one talk, offering a considerable amount of "evidence" of the distribution of Helium-3 in the atmosphere, which was allegedly caused by the pre-Flood vapor canopy collapsing. But in the public question time, one student, who was himself a creationist, queried this, on the grounds that many creationists do not accept the canopy theory any more. Indeed, I no longer accept the canopy theory[2], so all my previous "evidence" in support of it flies out of the window. As I have suggested in an earlier chapter, it is not that I won't use evidence anymore. It is simply that the evidence must be used in the context of our presuppositions. This is the line that Ken Ham has been advocating for years, and it is why I consider him to be one of the foremost Presuppositional Apologists. If I may paraphrase Ken, he has described it like this. We present evidence that evolution is not true. The evolutionists goes away, and comes back with some "better" evidence. So, we have to find other evidence, to counteract that new evidence. And so on! It is far more efficient, as well as more logically and biblically sound, to attack the evolutionist's presupposition, showing that they are interpreting evidence through a false filter, while we are building our case on a solid foundation, and interpreting the evidence based on that solid foundation.

The truth is that creationists have been very guilty in the past of using Evidential Apologetics, or Classical Apologetics, instead of illustrating presuppositions.

I am the Director of the Mount St Helens Creation Center, in Toutle, Washington state. I take people on full day excursions around the volcano and the areas associated with the 1980 eruptions. It is very tempting to present the volcano as very strong evidence that the world did not take millions of years to form in the way that it did. Indeed, I can and do show people where there are layers of sediments, 200 or more layers, and over 25 ft thick, which formed in the space of three hours.

But does this "prove" that the world's sedimentary layers formed in the same way? I suggest to you that it does not. That is not the way our discussion should proceed. Instead, I talk to people about the events of the Flood, and how there were volcanic, seismic and sedimentary activities. I can then show them that the formations at Mount St Helens are consistent with the biblical account. Indeed, they are what we would expect, if the biblical Flood account were true (which it is). They are not what we would expect, if the paradigm of millions-of-years were true. It is a very subtle difference in style and tone, but I hope you get the point. I am probably one of the few creationists, who has been leading excursions around Mount St Helens, who does so in a presuppositional manner.

Young Earth Creationist

I dislike the term Young Earth Creationist. The Earth is not young. The earth is very, very old. It is as much as 6,000 years old. 6,000 years is a long time, and cannot be called old.

Of course, when people describe themselves as Young Earth Creationists, they mean that the earth is young compared to the evolutionary millions of years. But why should I define myself, according to a presupposition that I do not accept. For that reason, I tend not to use the term Young Earth Creationist very often. I prefer *Biblical Creationist*.

The existence of the term Young Earth Creationist has led to some unfortunate errors in creationism. Creationists wedded to Classical Apologetics are mostly interested in opposing the theory of evolution, and its associated millions of years. Therefore, most people who describe themselves as Young Earth Creationists hold to an age of the Earth, up to about 10,000 years. In fact, some go further. One prominent so-called Young Earth Creationist organization in the UK accepts an age for the Earth of up to 30,000 years. I have even heard one YEC state that the Earth could be a million years old.

In my little book, *the Biblical Age of the Earth*[3], I have shown how the age of the Earth is calculated from verses in the Bible. Some YECs have expressed horror at this, citing certain scientific processes that take longer than 6,000 years. What they fail to realize is that they are adopting false and unbiblical presuppositions, in order to make these claims. The only reason for not accepting the chronology that I propose is to do with influences from outside of the Bible, and not from Scripture itself. Of course, I do not take credit for my chronology. I am simply verifying from Scripture what many notable "divines" of the past have inferred, most notably Archbishop James Ussher (1581 - 1656)[4]

Intelligent Design

The archetypal Classical Apologists most closely associated with creationism, at least in the minds of the public, are the advocates of the so-called *Intelligent Design Movement*. Advocates of ID seek to undermine people's belief in evolution.

They accept that evolution is a godless philosophy, so they use scientific methodology and theory, in order to oppose evolution.

One of the most famous examples of an ID idea is that of the flagellum motor in the e-coli bacterium. This nasty little bacterium (which causes food poisoning) has this fascinating long external organ, which it moves like a whip, or even like an outboard motor, to cause the organism to move. An article on one website describes the flagellum motor thus:

> *Over 40 different kinds of proteins make up the bacterial flagellum. These biomolecules function in concert as a literal rotary motor whose components include a rotor, stator, drive shaft, bushing, universal joint, and propeller. The bacterial flagellum is essentially a molecular-sized electrical motor (the flow of positively charged hydrogen ions through the motor proteins located in the bacterial inner membrane powers the flagellum's rotation) directly analogous to man-made rotary motors...*
>
> *In other words, the common design of the export apparatus and the F1-F0 ATP synthase [which causes the motor's structure] further adds to the stack of evidence for a Creator.*[5]

So far so good. The theory tells us that it is impossible for this organism to have evolved this system. That is a correct conclusion. Evolution is supposed to proceed by one mutation at a time, so the requirement for 40 favorable mutations at once is simply not possible. ID advocates therefore cite this structure as proof that evolution is wrong, and that some intelligence exists, which must have designed this organ.

However, I have hinted earlier that I am not impressed by an argument which "proves" the existence of a deity. I am interested in bringing people to know the true God of the Bible. For this reason, I chose carefully the website, from which I was going to take the quote. I have quoted from the Reasons to Believe website. Reasons to Believe is a ministry, led by Hugh Ross and Fazale Rana, which does not accept the literal truth of Genesis, believing in millions of years. But I could have drawn the quote from even worse websites. If all that we are trying to do is prove the existence of an Intelligent Designer, then who is this designer? Some in the ID movement believe in the God of the Bible, others are Muslims[6], others believe in various Hindu deities, and some can even believe that the intelligent designers were aliens from another planet.[7] (For a creationist analysis of the idea of extra-terrestrial aliens, please read Gary Bates's excellent book on the subject, *Alien Intrusion*)[8].

In fact, the arguments of the Intelligent Design Movement simply bring us back to the discussion that we had in Chapter

3. Since the Intelligent Designer proved by ID is a "probable" god, it is not a god at all, and is therefore a form of idolatry.

Does that mean that I would never discuss the flagellum motor in one of my creation presentations? It does not! I am happy to discuss it, and to quote the Intelligent Design advocate, who made such a big deal about it.[9] The difference is one of the starting point. Everything that I say is framed in the presupposition that God exists and the Bible is true, and I can therefore show that the difficulty evolutionists have with the flagellum motor is precisely what we would expect, given their presupposition, whereas it makes complete sense, given the correct biblical presuppositions.

Creationists need to learn this lesson over and over again. In my opinion, creationism is compelling. Evolution, even by secular presuppositions, is a weak theory, and it is easy to pick holes in it. Indeed, I have already stated on page 144 that evolution is not really a theory at all. So it is not too hard a task to convince someone that evolution is inadequate, or even wrong. And it is not too much harder to convince them, by intellect alone, that creationism, or at least ID, is correct. But if that is all I do, then that new, convinced creationist is still going to Hell. What matters is the Gospel of Jesus Christ. So it is to the important and inseparable relationship between apologetics and evangelism that I turn in the final chapter.

[1] Ham, K. (2010), *What's the Best "Proof" of Creation*, in ed. Ham, K. *New Answers Book 2*, online edition, < https://answersingenesis.org/evidence-for-creation/whats-the-best-proof-of-creation/ >, retrieved 1/16/2016

[2] If you want to know why I do not accept the canopy theory, read this article. Taylor, P.F. (2012), *Explaining the Flood without the Canopy*, < http://creationtoday.org/explaining-the-flood-without-the-canopy/ >, retrieved 1/16/2016

[3] Taylor, P.F. (2015), *The Biblical Age of the Earth*, J6D Publications

[4] Ussher, J. (1660 posthumous), *The Annals of the World*, (update version 2007, Master Books)

[5] Rana, F. (2011), *Bacterial Flagellum Structure Stacks the Case for Intelligent Design*, (Reasons to Believe), < http://www.reasons.org/articles/bacterial-flagellum-structure-stacks-the-case-for-intelligent-design >, retrieved 1/16/2016

[6] I do not accept that Allah in the Quran is the same as the true God of the Bible. See Slick, M., *Is Allah, the God of Islam, the same as the Yahweh the God of the Bible?*, < https://carm.org/god-islam-christianity-same >, retrieved 1/16/2016

[7] The very strange website referenced here is that of the RAEL cult, who believe in a sort of worship of "aliens" from outer space. I do not recommend studying the website, but

include it to prove a point. If you are concerned about extra-terrestrial issues, I recommend you read the book in the next reference. < http://www.rael.org/message >, retrieved 1/16/2016

[8] Bates, G. (2010 2nd edition), *Alien Intrusion: UFOs and the Evolution Connection*, (Creation book Publishers)

[9] Behe, M. (2006 2nd edn), *Darwin's Black Box*, (Free Press)

13 Treasures of Wisdom

Pilate therefore said to Him, "Are You a king then?" Jesus answered, "You say rightly that I am a king. For this cause I was born, and for this cause I have come into the world, that I should bear witness to the truth. Everyone who is of the truth hears My voice." Pilate said to Him, "What is truth?" And when he had said this, he went out again to the Jews, and said to them, "I find no fault in Him at all.[1]

Jesus, before Pilate, said that He had come "that I should bear witness to the truth". He continued, by saying that those who were of the truth would hear Him, and, by inference, understand Him. I may be in danger of reading too much into the text with my next words, but I notice that Pilate asked "What is truth?", but did not stick around for the answer. It is probably safe to say that Pilate was not one of those who were "of the truth". Perhaps these words from his Gospel were still in his mind, years later, when the apostle John wrote:

We are of God. He who knows God hears us; he who is not of God does not hear us. By this we know the spirit of truth and the spirit of error.[2]

Jesus had said before that those "of the truth" would hear His voice. John then says that "we are of God", and "He who knows God hears us; he who is not of God does not hear us."

The parallel is remarkable. Truth is found in God. Being "of the truth" is the same as being "of God", because God is Truth. This would be further evidence that Pilate was completely without God. First, he asks "what is truth?". Second, he does not wait for the answer, suggesting that he was not interested in the answer. In fact, every time I read that portion of John's Gospel, I am hit again and again by how grotesquely cynical was Pilate's rhetorical question. His words show that he knew Jesus was innocent, yet he did not care, because truth, to him, was an abstraction, rather than a concrete, absolute reality.

Absolute Truth

One of the corollaries of the Presuppositional Apologetic that we have outlined is the fact that absolute truth exists. This is a completely biblical and logical point. Our opponents might say "absolute truth does not exist", but, by so saying, they contradict themselves, because that statement is a statement of absolute knowledge. This is ever recurring, because they may allow themselves this: that the statement "absolute truth does not exist" is the only statement of absolute knowledge that they will allow. But, by so saying, they have, in fact, made a second statement of absolute knowledge.

The Bible is clear that absolute truth does indeed exist, and is personified by God Himself. Truth is that factual basis, which accords with the character of God. Lying is forbidden in the Ten Commandments, and the reason why lying is wrong is because God is not a liar.

"God is not a man, that He should lie, Nor a son of man, that He should repent. Has He said, and will He not do? Or has He spoken, and will He not make it good?[1]

Having said that truth is personified by God, we can say specifically that our understanding of truth is as exemplified in the Second Person of the Trinity, Jesus Christ, the Son. And that, I believe, is what Jesus was getting at in His response to Pilate, recorded under inspiration by John for our benefit.

The Office of the Apologist

Reading the offices of the church listed in Ephesians 4, we do not find the word apologist. Without entering any sort of argument over which offices may or may not exist today, we certainly cannot find Apologist among them. Of course, there is no suggestion in Ephesians 4 that every Christian should have one of these offices. I think that most do not. But if an Apologist could be considered some sort of "appointment" by God, then it would have to be included under one of the headings of Ephesians 4. I suggest that the role of an Apologist is probably best understood as part of the role of the Evangelist, or the Teacher. There is certainly a role for apologetics in preaching. But, perhaps, its most obvious role is as part of the armory of the Evangelist.

In one conference, I shared a platform with a much better-known apologist. His job was to present Classical Apologetics, and mine to present Presuppositional Apologetics. At one point, this apologist described the role of the apologist as "pre-evangelism" - getting people ready for evangelism. To me, this concept is reminiscent of the evidential creationist, to which I referred in the previous chapter. What purpose is there in making a robust defense of the faith, if the one who is wavering, by the strength of your defense, does not hear the Gospel? Despite the fact that I have never thought that my primary gifting is that of an evangelist, I cannot see the purpose of separating apologetics from evangelism. The defense of the faith is valueless, if not accompanied by an account of how the hearer might be saved.

Mars Hill Again

One model that we can follow is that of the apostle Paul at Mars Hill. We have already looked at this account in Acts 17, but let's turn to it again.

> *Then Paul stood in the midst of the Areopagus and said, "Men of Athens, I perceive that in all things you are very religious; for as I was passing through and considering the objects of your worship, I even found an altar with this inscription: TO THE UNKNOWN GOD. Therefore, the One whom you worship without knowing, Him I proclaim to you: God, who made the world and everything in it, since He is Lord of heaven and earth, does not dwell in temples made with hands. Nor is He worshiped with men's hands, as though He needed anything, since He gives to all life, breath, and all*

things. And He has made from one blood every nation of men to dwell on all the face of the earth, and has determined their preappointed times and the boundaries of their dwellings, so that they should seek the Lord, in the hope that they might grope for Him and find Him, though He is not far from each one of us; for in Him we live and move and have our being, as also some of your own poets have said, 'For we are also His offspring.' Therefore, since we are the offspring of God, we ought not to think that the Divine Nature is like gold or silver or stone, something shaped by art and man's devising. Truly, these times of ignorance God overlooked, but now commands all men everywhere to repent, because He has appointed a day on which He will judge the world in righteousness by the Man whom He has ordained. He has given assurance of this to all by raising Him from the dead."[1]

We have already commented on how Paul's Mars Hill address is an example of apologetics. But it is also an example of evangelism. Having given a robust background to his apologetic, Paul concludes by calling for repentance and faith in Jesus, while warning of judgment. His apologetics swings naturally into evangelism. Paul's purpose was always to share the Gospel, rather than to score debating points.

Weakness, Fear and Trembling

Paul is one of the most remarkable characters in the Bible. We know little about his upbringing. However, everything that we find out about him proves to be a surprise.

Obviously, he is a Jew. He is of the tribe of Benjamin. But he is also a Pharisee, well versed in the ecclesiastical law and traditions of the time, having studied under Gamalial. We know that he was not convinced of Christianity by human means. In fact, he began by persecuting the church, until he was miraculously saved on the road to Damascus, by a vision of Jesus Christ. His reputation as a fierce persecutor of Christians was so great, that the early church was understandably fearful of him, when he came to them as a converted believer. And this remarkable man was not just a Jew; he was also legally a Roman citizen, having inherited this prized citizenship from his father. His knowledge of the Old Testament Scriptures was immense. He wrote so much about what Jesus did that we must assume that, as a non-witness, he had conversed with and carefully listened to what Jesus' disciples had to say. And we discover in Acts 17 that he even had an encyclopedic grasp of Greek poetry.

With this sort of background, we could imagine that his debating and oratorical skills would have been finely tuned. He could probably have knocked spots off any opponent in a debate, including formal Greek debates. Yet, when he referred to his own style of ministry, in his first letter to the church at

Corinth, it is clear that he was in the habit of restraining himself, and limiting this vast intellect, in order to be humble.

> *And I, brethren, when I came to you, did not come with excellence of speech or of wisdom declaring to you the testimony of God. For I determined not to know anything among you except Jesus Christ and Him crucified. I was with you in weakness, in fear, and in much trembling. And my speech and my preaching were not with persuasive words of human wisdom, but in demonstration of the Spirit and of power, that your faith should not be in the wisdom of men but in the power of God.*[1]

This humility and care is a model for us. Few of us can aspire to the heights of achievement to which Paul had risen, yet even that which we have can be used for wrong effect, if we do not have Paul's weakness, fear and trembling. His motivation was that people would not concentrate on him, but on God. He thought their faith "should not be in the wisdom of men but in the power of God."

Gentleness and Respect

I once had a word cloud produced from my book "The Six Days of Genesis". This is a diagram, showing a lot of words, with differently sized typography. The larger the font, the more frequently that word appears in the book. Having recently read Voddie Baucham's excellent book *Expository*

Apologetics[1], I thought that if a word cloud were made from that book, one of the largest letter sizes would be for the word *winsome*. Baucham uses that word liberally. I had to look it up, though I sort-of knew what it meant. I just needed an exact dictionary definition. Websters defines winsome as:

> *Generally pleasing and engaging often because of a childlike charm and innocence.*[2]

Baucham kept using the word, as a corrective to the way that many of us do apologetics. I notice an occasional aggressive tendency on Facebook, where there are some who rejoice in the idea of putting atheists down hard, when Baucham tells us we should be "winsome".

> *In your hearts honor Christ the Lord as holy, always being prepared to make a defense to anyone who asks you for a reason for the hope that is in you; yet do it with gentleness and respect.*[3]

We talked earlier about having this verse used in its proper context. So let's close out by looking at that context again.

The famous phrase in this verse is this: "always be prepared to make a defense to anyone who asks you for a reason for the hope that is in you". Yet this phrase is sandwiched between two others that we must not miss.

"In your hearts honor Christ the Lord as holy". Some versions tell us to set apart the Lord, or to sanctify Him. All these mean the same thing. To be holy is to be set apart and to be sanctified. Therefore, we notice that the whole purpose of apologetics is to be Christ-centered. Of course, you might object that I have chosen the ESV for this quotation, instead of my usual NKJV, because the latter does not include the word Christ. Yet the word Christ is clearly implied in the NKJV, if you read what is to come in verse 16, which is why I am not worried about its omission, and why I feel I am justified in using the ESV at this point to hammer it home.

So, the first slice of bread for the apologetic sandwich is honoring Christ as holy. The other slice of bread is this: "do it with gentleness and respect". The NKJV's "meekness and fear" is equally valid. And I am sure that these can be neatly summarized by using the word "winsome".

You see, this verse actually forbids using Presuppositional Apologetics as a Hulk-Loki method. That will disappoint many (and make others angry). The Facebook Presuppers all seem to love this muscular, testosterone-filled theology, and most of them, for obvious reasons, seem to be young men. But I am not arguing for the feminization of apologetics. Far from it. No one could accuse Paul's methods or Peter's methods of being feminized. They are robust, firm, well-thought through, and relevant, but they are also winsome. Why? Because both these apostles have a motivation, which does not consist in winning arguments for the sake of winning arguments. Instead, their whole *raison d' être* is, where possible, to bring people to Christ, so they might repent and be saved.

That should also be our motivation.

Wisdom and Christ

In chapter 4, we saw that wisdom is really a personification of Jesus. Hence, in drawing together everything about both wisdom and knowledge, Paul says:

> *In whom [Christ] are hidden all the treasures of wisdom and knowledge.*[i]

This book has been all about the true place of concepts such as knowledge, wisdom, truth, and absolute authority. This verse, and others we have studied, tell us that all these things are found in Christ. So apologetics should certainly include the Gospel, and apologetics should probably be a key tool used in evangelism. The purpose of apologetics is to bring people to Christ. And that purpose is founded on the presupposition that God exists and His Word is True.

Nothing else is necessary. No evidence is required, or even permitted, for your faith. Jesus says to you, along with Jairus, "Only Believe".

[1] John 18:37-38

[2] 1 John 4:6

[1] Numbers 23:19

[1] Acts 17:22-31

[1] 1 Corinthians 2:1-5

[1] Baucham, V. (2015), *Expository Apologetics*, (Crossway) - you must get this book

[2] "Winsome." Merriam-Webster.com. Merriam-Webster, n.d. Web. 16 Jan. 2016.

[3] 1 Peter 3:15 (ESV)

[1] Colossians 2:3

Appendix: Deconstructing Dawkins

In 2006, Richard Dawkins published his famous book, *The God Delusion*. Intended to be the last word in atheism, the book shot holes through the traditional atheist position of gently ignoring religion, and stood up as an example of popular atheism at its most evangelistic.

When Dawkins published his book, I put together a presentation in response. I have been asked to put down a written version of the presentation, so it seemed appropriate to include it here. However, it is not really part of the argument about the methodology of apologetics, so I have placed it here as an appendix.

At the time, Dawkins was the Simonyi Professor for the Public Understanding of Science at the University of Oxford; a position which he held from 1995 through 2008. The chair, funded by an endowment from programmer, entrepreneur and philanthropist Charles Simonyi, was specially created for Dawkins, who had previously been (and, still is) a Fellow at New College, Oxford, as a teacher and researcher in zoology. His popularising style caused him to be in demand with the media, who are justifiably attracted to professional scientists, who can be understood by the general public. He had, for example, presented the Royal Institution Christmas Lectures for Children in 1991 - a prestigious annual program, initiated in 1825 by Michael Faraday, and hosted by Faraday on 19 occasions. Quite what Faraday - an evangelical Christian, arguably Britain's greatest ever scientist, and skeptic of the new-fangled Darwinian ideas - would have made of an evolutionary atheist filling his seat, we can only speculate.

Even before 1995, Dawkins had been known publicly to air his atheism. He has also been an ardent critic of creationism, describing it as "a preposterous, mind-shrinking falsehood".[1] In 2006, he presented a pair of documentary films on Britain's Channel 4 network, entitled *The Root of all Evil*, in which he argued that pretty much everything wrong in today's society is due to the presence of religion. While he claimed to be criticizing religion in general, he was, in fact, criticizing Christianity in particular.

So, the publication of Dawkins's anti-theist polemic was eagerly awaited. Although I did not, by any means, expect that *The God Delusion* was going to shake my faith, I did at least anticipate that there might be some challenges to face. I thought I might have some real meat to get my teeth into, in order to produce an apologetic against it. I have to admit that I was quite disappointed that the book was as weak as I believe it to be. The tone of the book is angry, and anger does not lead to good argument. The level of argument can be found from this excerpt (which was also quoted in chapter 3).

> *The God of the Old Testament is arguably the most unpleasant character in all fiction: jealous and proud of it; a petty, unjust, unforgiving control-freak; a vindictive, bloodthirsty ethnic cleanser; a misogynistic, homophobic, racist, infanticidal, genocidal, filicidal, pestilential, megalomaniacal, sadomasochistic, capriciously malevolent bully.[2]*

The passage quoted can be said to have a certain poetry about it, and it always seems to get a cheer whenever Dawkins reads it publicly. But stringing together words in a clever formation does not constitute and argument.

I would submit that the person with the delusion is Dawkins himself. Indeed, I have noticed two delusions in the book. The first concerns his use of Scripture, because he actually quotes from the Bible a lot. The second is in his use, or abuse, of logic.

Dawkins's Use of Scripture

When I first read *The God Delusion*, I was a little surprised to see how much Scripture Dawkins quotes. And yet, when he is quoting Scripture, he takes it out of context, because he does not appear to have read it in context. Indeed, his use of Bible texts is a major weakness of the book. One would have thought that, if one were to write a book denigrating the Bible, that one would have carefully read what the Bible actually said.

This would be particularly important for a scholar like Richard Dawkins. He does not seem to like the idea of non-biologists pontificating on the subject of evolution, yet he feels quite happy to plow into theorizing on the Bible, while he remains ignorant of much of its content and structure.

Presuppositions of Morality

In the passage from Dawkins's book quoted above, he makes a couple of moral judgments about God. Let me look at two of them. He judges that God is a nasty character, because he is homophobic. Given the popular use of the word (meaning someone opposed to homosexuality, rather than someone afraid of homosexuals), why would Dawkins not expect the Bible to reveal God as being opposed to homosexuality? In his diatribe, Dawkins does not explain what his evidence is for suggesting that homosexuality is an acceptable practice. The fact that it is currently culturally acceptable is not sufficient, in a book, which claims to be analyzing the existence of God by the scientific method. Whether something is right or wrong is not defined by the whim of the culture. The only way that someone can imply that a particular practice is morally right or wrong is by appealing to an absolute standard - and the only absolute standard of morality we have is the Bible. So Dawkins borrows from a biblical concept, in order to criticize a biblical concept.

Dawkins also accuses God of being a control freak. This, however, is an illogical claim. It is a category error. Dawkins is attempting to impose an outside culture on a cultural reference, where it is not warranted. If he had really read the Bible, he would have realized that the Hebrew concept of ownership is by creation.

"Whose is that boat?"

"It's Peter's boat"

"Why is it Peter's boat?"

"Because he made it".

In the same way, God has every right to be in control, because He is the Creator. If I try to control people, that would be control-freakery! But when God does it, it is not, because we are dealing with a different category.

Ignorance of History

Dawkins also demonstrates, in his use of Scripture, a failure to read biblical history. For example, he claims that Jesus did not claim to be God.

> *The historical evidence that Jesus claimed any sort of divine status is minimal.*[3]

This is not the case. The evidence is pretty overwhelming. We are sometimes hampered, in spotting the evidence, by the language barrier. For example, the New Testament was written in Koine Greek. The Old Testament was written in Hebrew. Jesus would probably have spoken Aramaic, which is sufficiently similar to Hebrew for this next point to be valid.

In Exodus 3:14, God revealed to Moses, though the burning bush, His Divine Name.

> And God said to Moses, "I AM WHO I AM." And He said, "Thus you shall say to the children of Israel, 'I AM has sent me to you.' "

The Divine Name is this revealed to be "I AM". In Hebrew, this is represented by four Hebrew letters, which approximate to the Latin letters YHWH. It is not clear how to pronounce this. Most experts today pronounce it *Yaheweh*. In times past, it was often mistakenly pronounced *Jehovah*. But in most English translations, it is represented in the Old Testament by the word LORD, where four capital letters are used. So, we can make this equaltion:

I AM = YHWH = LORD

Psalm 23 begins "The LORD is my shepherd". So this is really "I AM is my shepherd". So, in John 10:11, when Jesus said "I am the Good Shepherd", all the people listening to Him knew exactly what He was saying. Jesus was unambiguously and openly claiming to be God. We have had to do detective work in English to reach this conclusion. But the people listening to Jesus would not have had that problem. Jesus' meaning could not be confused for anything else.

Here is another of Dawkins's claims.

> In any case, if Jesus really was born of a virgin, Joseph's ancestry is irrelevant and cannot be used to fulfill, on Jesus' behalf, the Old Testament prophecy that the Messiah should be descended from David.[4]

Dawkins clearly shows that he misunderstands the point of Joseph's ancestry. Plus, Joseph's ancestry is not the only one we have. In Luke 3, we have a genealogy though Jesus' mother Mary.[5] The reason we know that this is Mary's ancestry, is because of the little use of the definite article when describing Joseph's sonship in Luke 3.

God had promised that one of David's sons would be on the throne forever.

> When your days are fulfilled and you rest with your fathers, I will set up your seed after you, who will come from your body, and I will establish his kingdom. He shall build a house for My name, and I will establish the throne of his kingdom forever.[6]

However, the promise given to David's son Solomon was not unconditional.

> *Therefore the LORD said to Solomon, "Because you have done this, and have not kept My covenant and My statutes, which I have commanded you, I will surely tear the kingdom away from you and give it to your servant. Nevertheless I will not do it in your days, for the sake of your father David; I will tear it out of the hand of your son. However I will not tear away the whole kingdom; I will give one tribe to your son for the sake of My servant David, and for the sake of Jerusalem which I have chosen."[7]*

Solomon disobeyed God, so he did indeed lose the kingdom for his descendents, except the new Southern kingdom of Judah, comprising of the tribes of Judah and Benjamin. Eventually, God removed the last of Solomon's line.

> *28 "Is this man Coniah [Jehoiachin] a despised, broken idol--A vessel in which is no pleasure? Why are they cast out, he and his descendants, And cast into a land which they do not know?*

> *29 O earth, earth, earth, Hear the word of the LORD!*

> *30 Thus says the LORD: 'Write this man down as childless, A man who shall not prosper in his days; For none of his*

descendants shall prosper, Sitting on the throne of David, And

ruling anymore in Judah."[8]

However, the promise to David was still unconditional.

The LORD has sworn in truth to David;

He will not turn from it:

"I will set upon your throne the fruit of your body.

If your sons will keep My covenant

And My testimony which I shall teach them,

Their sons also shall sit upon your throne forevermore."[9]

So, the Messiah had to be descended from David, but not from Solomon. Joseph was descended from Solomon, so could not be the literal, human father of Jesus. However, Jesus inherited His Davidic kingship through another of David's sons - Nathan - because Mary was a descendent of Nathan. Joseph's legal descent from Solomon also adds to Jesus' kingship, even though the literal kingship had been removed from that line.

There are many other criticisms of Dawkins's use of Scripture that could be mentioned. In my talk, I show how Dawkins criticizes people getting their morality from the Bible, by citing the account in Judges 19 of the Levite and the concubine. This couple arrive at a town in Benjamin, where the people want to commit homosexual rape on the Levite, but settle for gang-raping the concubine.

Dawkins does not understand that this account is not teaching that either side in the dispute were moral. In fact, that whole sordid story has no heroes. The Levite should not have had a concubine. The people should not have wanted to violate the Levite. The Levite had no right to allow the men of the town to use his concubine. No one in that story appears to be righteous. The Bible is not taking sides - it is reporting what actually happened. The moral of the story is the oft repeated refrain in Judges "In those days, Israel had no king, and everyone did as he pleased". Of course, Israel was supposed to have a king. God was their King! The whole point of the latter half of Judges is a sordid tale of what happens to as society that refuses to follow God's law.

Dawkins's Logic

A logical fallacy is an attempt to make a logical argument, which is unsound - i.e. conclusions do not follow directly from premises, or the premises themselves may be incorrect.

The God Delusion is surprisingly full of logical fallacies. Indeed, I could teach a whole course on logical fallacies, illustrating every one from *The God Delusion*. Here are a few.

Circular Reasoning

Circular reasoning (and I am specifically referring to "vicious circular reasoning", sometimes called "begging the question") occurs when one of the premises is actually the conclusion which is supposed to be being proved. This might sound obviously wrong, but a circular argument is not necessarily immediately obvious. For instance, here is Dawkins's "proof" that no intelligent designer could have made the universe.

Creative intelligences, being evolved, necessarily arrive late in the universe, and therefore cannot be responsible for designing it.[10]

This is circular. In order to prove evolution, Dawkins has started by assuming evolution.

Ad Hominem

This is when an argument is rejected, based on criticizing the quality of the person making the argument. For example:

He moved up the hierarchy of American universities, from rock bottom at the "Moody Bible Institute", through Wheaton College (a little bit higher on the scale, but still the alma mater of Billy Graham) to Princeton in the world-beating class at the top.[11]

Notice the insulting comments about Moody Bible Institute and Wheaton College. In soccer terms, we often call this playing the man instead of playing the ball. It is like when a tackle is made by the opposing player kicking the shin deliberately instead of the ball.

Appeal to Authority

This is when an argument is deemed to be true, because of the status of the arguer. Read this example.

The nineteenth century is the last time when it was possible for an educated person to admit to believing in miracles like the virgin birth without embarrassment.

Notice that this statement is defining an "educated person" as someone who does not believe in miracles.

Conclusion

In my talk on *Deconstructing Dawkins*, I give several other examples of the poor use of Scripture and the poor use of Logic.

In conclusion, we see that there is actually nothing to fear from *The God Delusion*. Its arguments are weak. It does not contain a reasoned argument. We also see that a presupposition of the truth of the Bible is a completely intellectually satisfying position to take. Reason and logic flow naturally, from a starting point, which involves believing the Bible to be inspired, inerrant and authoritative. That is why Paul reminds us, in Romans 12:2, that we are to "Be transformed by the renewing of your mind".

[1] Dawkins, R. (2002), *A Scientist's View*, The Guardian, < http://www.theguardian.com/uk/2002/mar/09/religion.schools1 >, retrieved 1/17/2016

[2] Dawkins, R. (2006), *The God Delusion*, (Mariner), p31

[3] p92

[4] p95

[5] Fruchtenbaum, A.G. (2005), *Yeshua's Right to David's Throne*, < http://www.messianicassociation.org/ezine12-David'sThrone.htm >, retrieved February 8th 2016

[6] 2 Samuel 7:12-13

[7] 1 Kings 11:11-13

[8] Jeremiah 22:29-30

[9] Psalm 132:11-12

[10] p31

[11] p95

Where Birds Eat Horses helps you spot the pseudo-scientific language used by evolutionists. The subtitle is "The Language of Evolution", and the book shows how the "evidence" for evolution consists not in scientific experiment, but in the clever and deceptive use of language. Learn how to spot fuzzy words, magic words, and false presuppositions.

"Paul has penned yet another stellar defense of the biblical account of creation. You must have this book!" **Carl Gallups**

"Paul Taylor is uniquely gifted with insight into this groundless and godless philosophy. May God use this book to equip millions." **Ray Comfort**

Available from Amazon, Mount St Helens Creation Center (mshcreationcenter.org), and wherever books are sold.

Doctrine is not something that is cold. It should be alive and vibrant. It is relevant, because it links the teaching of the Bible to everyday situations.

Most Christian doctrines are based on a foundation of Genesis. Paul Taylor has taken some of those teachings that matter to us most - the Trinity, the Deity of Christ, the Inerrancy of Scripture, Sin and Death, Salvation, Faith and Abraham and the Second Coming. In an easy to follow style, he looks at what the Bible says about each teaching, and then shows that it is much easier to understand and accept each teaching, when we start by believing the early chapters of Genesis to be true.

Available from Amazon, Mount St Helens Creation Center (mshcreationcenter.org), and wherever books are sold.

Itching Ears

How the most important Christian doctrines are rooted in Genesis

Paul F Taylor

The two epistles to the Thessalonians contain much of the basic, biblical teaching on the End Times. For this reason, they have often been controversial. Yet the material they contain is essential for anyone who wants to get to grips with this subject, as well as providing an insight into the establishment of a church, which the apostle Paul commends as behaving exactly as a church should.

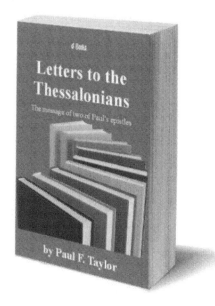

Paul Taylor argues that a literal reading of these epistles leads one to a Historic (Posttribulation) Premillennial understanding of the End Times.

Available from Amazon, Mount St Helens Creation Center (mshcreationcenter.org), and wherever books are sold.

The Creation Caching website was a major project for Paul Taylor's web development agency - Old Castle Web Solutions. It involved writing two new plugins and two new themes for a Wordpress installation.

This book is the story of how these technologies were put together, to achieve the website. The code for the various components can be obtained from:

www.oldcastleweb .com

Join a web developer in action, to see how this sort of coding happens.

Made in the USA
San Bernardino, CA
18 February 2016